Throughout my baseball career I saw many talented players abort what could've been Hall of Fame careers because they were deficient in patience which eventually deterred them from their divine destiny. Jeffery insightfully gives us this brilliant resource that teaches us the powerful truth that sometimes God's strategy is delay. When embraced, that delay propels you into your divine assignment.

—Mariano Rivera
New York Yankees Unanimous 1ˢᵗ Ballot Hall of Famer,
MLB All-Time Saves Leader
5X World Series Champion

Dr. Jeffery Portmann combines his life experience and Biblical principles to remind you that God's dream for your destiny is bigger than your dream, and that He accomplishes His purposes with you from the inside out. The journey of reading "Delayed Destiny" will be well worth your time.

—Doug Clay
General Superintendent of The Assemblies of God

If you, like me, find yourself straining at the leash of time, struggling valiantly but vainly against the iron grip of those pesky, slow-moving clock hands, then Jeffery Portmann's excellent book, *Delayed Destiny*, is your next important read. With engaging stories and relatable metaphors that will keep you nodding in agreement, Jeffery points us to the life of the biblical character, Joseph, to unpack fresh truths about the vital things God is up to in those agonizing seasons of waiting—and why it matters how we respond. Further, he gives us practical spiritual strategies to wait actively and with hope. Here's a little advice to my fellow-waiters: don't delay reading this book—your God-planned destiny *will* come, just in time.

—Dr. Jodi Detrick
former columnist for *The Seattle Times*
Author of *The Jesus-Hearted Woman*
and *The Settled Soul: Tenaciously Abiding with a Tender God*

Most photos today are taken on smart phones and then viewed instantly. I remember when pictures were taken and then we had to wait for them to be developed in the dark room. God develops our destiny the same way. This new book, *Delayed Destiny*, by Dr. Jeffery Portmann will encourage you to trust and rest in the hands of the Master developer of destiny.

—Bishop Walter Harvey
President, National Black Fellowship of the Assemblies of God
Author of *Alley-Oop: Keys to Pastor Succession*

God has a divine destiny prepared for you. Your challenge is discovering that destiny and developing the patience necessary to remain faithful while waiting for the opportunity to step into it. In this book, Portmann draws on sound Biblical truths to offer practical tools to equip you to do just that. This is a must-read book for anyone who feels their ultimate destiny is being delayed. It's a gift from God to empower your life with purpose, meaning, and significance.

—Dr. Kent J. Ingle
President, Southeastern University
Author of *Framework Leadership*

"Slow motion is still motion." Wow! I believe Jeffery's new book will encourage your ministry in a time where we are questioning ourselves and our future. *Delayed Destiny* is going to provoke and disturb status. A must read for everyone involved in leadership!"

—Dr. Wilfredo "Choco" De Jesus
Assemblies of God General Treasurer
Author of *Love Them Anyway*

Jeffery masterfully debunks the myth and delusion that waiting and losing are synonymous. This modern classic will teach us the value of taking a knee & losing a round in order to win the fight and come out victorious.

—Pastor Mark Vega
Pastor Evangelist Ignite Life Center
Author of *Don't Wait For Me To Die*

It is an honor to write this endorsement for Dr. Jeffery Portmann's new book, "Delayed Destiny" as I have watched him live out these principles. This book will be a paper coach to you when facing discouragement, and you will. The single leadership nutrient laced in every page of this book is HOPE. Hope we can win. Hope we can succeed. Hope we can do what Jesus has assigned. Jeffery has tapped into the words of I Thess. 1:3 that "hope inspires endurance" and the practical suggestions and stories will give you exactly that…HOPE. I sincerely wish I'd had this book while leading our church's Turnaround in Seattle.

—Dr. Donald E. Ross
Northwest Ministry Network Leader
Author of *Turnaround Pastor*

We have all had seasons where we feel lost or stuck. The dream isn't happening as fast as you wanted it to. *Delayed Destiny* addresses these seasons head on. It might be slow, but it is significant and will move you towards your destiny. Thank you Jeffery Portmann for this crucial book.

—Dr. Aaron Burke
Lead Pastor Radiant Church Tampa, FL.

Portmann's thoughtful insights and encouragement will change the way you think and have you eagerly anticipating your delays, recognizing them as the building blocks to push you forward into your destiny. Don't just buy this book, read it, study it, and put it into action.

—Scott Wilson
Founder/CEO 415 Leaders, RSG Leaders
Global Pastor, Oaks Church
Author of *Identity: the Search for True Success and Significance*

If you feel like God is taking too long to fulfill his purposes for your life, then *Delayed Destiny* is a must-read book!

—Wes Davis
Lead Pastor newlife.tv
Author of *Jesus Apprentice*

In a culture full of hurry, instant results and immediate gratification Jeffery's message is not only refreshing but downright the heart of God. A must read!! One of the deceptions of social media is everyone loves the hype and success. No one is talking about slow and delayed. Yet it is in the slowdowns God provides us rest for our souls and fuel for our dreams

—Dr. Troy H. Jones
Lead Pastor New Life Renton
Founder *Recalibrate Group*
Author of *Recalibrate Your Church-*
How Your Church Can Reach It's Full Kingdom Impact

For the past 25 years I've had the privilege of having a front row seat into the life of Jeffery Portmann. I have spent countless hours with he and his family as well as traveling with him around the globe. The principles laid out in *Delayed Destiny* come from years of experience and wisdom which when applied will help you navigate your current season of life. Whether you are in a holding pattern waiting for what's next or in the most fulfilling season of your life, this book reminds you there is more on the other side of your delay.

—Justin Smith
National AG Next Gen Team

Have you ever noticed a discrepancy between your timeline and God's? In *Delayed Destiny*, Jeffery Portmann masterfully guides every driven leader trying to make sense of slowdowns. He explains both logically and theologically what God is up to in the delay. Jeffrey is a proven leader who is gifted at codifying his experience to instruct, inspire, and champion others. This book is right on time!

—Greg Ford
Lead Pastor One Church, Columbus, OH.

Portmann's practical and refreshing insight on how delays can actually serve to propel us not deter us is encouraging and applicable to all phases of life. This engaging study of Joseph's journey through difficult times reveals powerful truths that are sure to inspire us to not give up. This tool provides clarity, inspiration and an increased understanding that whatever we face is not greater than the favor and grace assigned to us by God. Your Destiny Is Worth The Delay.

—Michael Fernandez
Cornerstone Church, San Antonio TX.
Founder of *Impact Now*

Ever felt like your momentum, marriage, or ministry hit a sudden PAUSE? Jeffery Portmann's book utilizes a biblical framework to remind readers that in God's hands what might be perceived as "delays" with no direction, actually becoming developing moments, even in the midst of detours. This is an excellent resource providing practical tools for all leaders and pastors.

—Elly Marroquin
National Director of Christian Education & Discipleship

DELAYED

Embracing Slow Motion Growth

DESTINY

in a Fast Paced World

JEFFERY PORTMANN

Fedd Books
P.O. Box 341973
Austin, TX 78734
www.thefeddagency.com

Published in association with The Fedd Agency, Inc., a literary agency.

ISBN: 978-1-957616-13-1
eISBN: 978-1-957616-14-8

Library of Congress Number: 2022911401

Printed in the United States of America
First Edition 22 23 24 25 /6 5 4 3 2

*To my best friend and love, Joanne,
thank you for believing in me and bringing
out the best in us, especially when we're
experiencing delays in our destiny.
I dedicate this book to you.*

CONTENTS

Introduction vii

PART 1: WHAT HINDERS 1

  1: Distraction 3

  2: Detour 13

  3: Discontentment 23

  4: Discouragement 29

  5: Defensiveness 37

PART 2: WHAT HELPS 47

  6: What Helps 47

  7: Discernment 49

  8: Discovery 59

  9: Dependence 73

  10: Determination 83

  11: Development 93

Discussion Questions 113

INTRODUCTION

Slow Motion is Still Motion

Ever been in a season of life that seemed to lack forward momentum? You're doing everything possible to experience growth, maybe even repeating what's worked before. But then there's a moment, a month, or even an extended season where what you expected, hoped, and prayed for just isn't happening. You're in the midst of what I call a *delayed destiny*.

I've got good news and bad news. The bad news is that you'll never be done developing. Never. And that development rarely happens rapidly. What you want to see happen in your life and the lives of others, who you'll become, how you'll make this world a better place, the legacy you will leave—none of these things can be seen, experienced, or understood in a hurry.

But the good news is that God's not done. In fact, your delay can actually develop something epic in you which can have an eternal impact. I know that sounds melodramatic, but when we accepted Jesus' invitation to join his mission to bring the gospel to the world, we signed up to be part of something that had and still has eternal implications.

Sometimes we wonder and wander. Other times, we believe and become. This book is an invitation to believe that what you're navigating, though admittedly difficult at times, has the potential to produce something epic and eternal in you. It's often how God works: inside out, heart first.

In a short but significant letter, the Apostle Paul writes to a group of people he loves deeply. The city is Philippi, and his audience is fellow followers of Jesus. His writings would affirm what some already knew, while others would receive his words as an unexpected lifeline. If you've ever had to tread water for what seemed like forever, wondering if you'll be able to keep your head above the waves, only to be thrown a life ring just when you're ready to give up, you'll grasp the power of his words.

> It's often how God works: inside out, heart first.

After reminding the Philippians of his love for them and thanking God for their partnership in the gospel, Paul declares, "He who began a good work in you will be faithful to complete it" (Phil. 1:6). This simple fourteen-word sentence has lasting ramifications. Sometimes we just need someone we trust to remind us that things will be okay. That we're not too far gone. That the grasp of grace is still able to reach us.

Sometimes I just need to be reminded that the work taking place in my life is normal, and it's good. God is the originator and completer of that work. He brings the growth and ongoing development in us. Since He is a promise-maker and promise-keeper, there's confidence that accompanies this verse. His unchanging attributes further accentuate his continued work in us. That God is the same yesterday, today, and forever is only further cause for optimism. However, that good work regularly seems to take longer than we anticipate or prefer. As the book of Hebrews declares, no discipline seems pleasant at the time: it's painful in the moment. But later on, it produces a harvest of righteousness and peace for those who have been trained by it (Heb. 12:11). This book is about the *later on* and *those who are trained by it.*

Seasons of delay often seem at least to hinder our preferred future, next chapter, or breakthrough. At worst, these seasons hijack them completely, like something in the corner of your eye which still hasn't come into full view. In navigating through these seasons, we uncover valuable lessons mined from the most difficult moments. Every delay has the potential to develop your destiny.

Before we jump any deeper into this book, I want to remind you of one simple, yet reassuring truth that we'll keep coming back to: slow motion is still motion.

Between 1981 and 2011, the space agency NASA launched 135 missions aboard five different space shuttles. Every mission utilized a 6-million-pound machine called a crawler-transporter to haul the shuttles to their launch pads. At its inception, this machine was the largest ever created. It had to be gigantic to carry the 4.4-million-pound space shuttle, external tank, solid rocket boosters, and all the fuel.[1] This modern marvel had a top speed of one mile per hour when fully loaded. One. Mile. Per hour. Meanwhile, to reach the minimum altitude required to orbit the Earth, the space shuttle had to accelerate from zero to 18,000 miles per hour in eight and a half minutes.

> It is in navigating through these seasons that we uncover valuable lessons, mined from the most difficult moments.

The extremes are almost comical. That something with the capacity to travel 23.6 times the speed of sound would be delivered to the launch pad at the excruciating speed of one mile per hour is another glimpse of what seems initially like a delayed destiny.

Getting the space shuttle from its storage facility to the launch pad takes nearly 5 hours. During that trip, the crawler burns 150 gallons of diesel oil per mile. That's a lot. But we understand intuitively that one

---

1 Cool Cosmos, "How much did the Space Shuttle weigh?" https://coolcosmos.ipac.caltech.edu/ask/268-How-much-did-the-Space-Shuttle-weigh-.

trip allows the other trip to happen. The space shuttle doesn't get to see the stars until it has slowly made its way down the street. Our lives are no different. We want to go fast. But often, in order to go fast, we first have to go slow. It's a paradox that applies to all people.

If you think about it, most of the growth you've already experienced in life has been incremental. For some reason, we tend to think this rate of change will speed up. But it doesn't. Few things grow fast.

Take a moment to think about what's most significant in your life. What do you value? The most important things in my life are all connected to a relationship. First with Jesus, then my wife and kids (we have two sons and two daughters-in-love), and then with others. All of these relationships require intentionality for their cultivation, built on the slow progress of time. And time is one of the things our culture doesn't want to spend. But what happens when our perspective shifts from irritation at the delay to anticipation for development?

That's what I'd like to invite you to consider as you read further. The initial idea for this project came from a sermon series I wrote while a youth pastor outside of Seattle, Washington. I wanted to help hundreds of teens and young adults (and, if I'm being honest, myself) embrace the idea that our dreams of growing relationships and continued personal growth were worth the time and energy we were investing in them. That the development we desired was possible. One essential element had to be acknowledged along the way: this development wouldn't happen quickly. I don't know if you've ever felt like you should be farther along than you are, whether in your career, relationships, finances, or as a follower of Christ. Maybe you wonder why things keep progressing at a painfully slow pace. I know I sure have before. If you're surprised that you're not where you thought you'd be, you're not alone.

If you're surprised that you're not where you thought you'd be, you're not alone.

A Joseph Kind of Waiting

I believe the central theme of the scriptures is God's loving pursuit of and provision for his creation and our response. Over and over again, we see God initiating relationships with and setting in motion His will for humanity. We also observe an ongoing pattern of our embracing His goodness, walking with Him for a bit, developing an attitude of self-sufficiency, and then facing the consequences. Our sinful nature naturally drifts toward doing things our own way. Thank God that His nature is unwavering in its goodness and expression. Almost every Bible story displays elements of His patience and persistence in caring for His creation.

There are so many incredible characters scattered throughout the Bible. They are men and woman, young and old, courageous and fearful, faith-filled and disobedient—all of whom we get glimpses of as we turn the pages. One of my favorite Bible characters is a guy named Joseph. He's a key player in the Old Testament whose life points humanity to the coming Messiah. He's actually a *type of Christ*—which means he foreshadows what's to come in Jesus. His messy life story paints a picture of what would ultimately happen through the miracle of Christ. He would be the one whom God would strategically position to deliver the people.

In his lifetime, Joseph would be used to rescue people from starvation. In Joseph's journey, there would be seven years of abundance followed by a seven-year famine for Egypt and the surrounding nations. This famine devastated everyone it touched, and the people became desperate. Joseph's people experienced a literal hunger that mirrored humanity's spiritual hunger, which could only be filled by Jesus the Messiah. And Joseph was just one member of a family tree stretching back past Jacob and Isaac—all the way to Abraham. It was Abraham who received the promise of God's salvation, but Joseph and his people were still waiting for its fulfillment—and would keep waiting—generations later.

One of the things I most appreciate about Joseph's story is that it's real and raw. If we're not careful, we can read or think about biblical characters with an inaccurate understanding of their reality. It's easy to assume that their lives looked and felt a lot different from ours. In a matter of minutes, we read a chapter or two that describes their lives, forgetting that in real time, these chapters played out over months, years, and even decades. What we discover in looking honestly at their lives is that you and I have something in common with each of them. In addition to all the miracles and milestones, they experienced disappointment, discouragement, and delays.

In its simplest form, the story of Joseph is a front-row seat to God's divine providence. Joseph experienced what I call a delayed destiny. And even with divine intervention, the chapters of his life unfold slowly, more painfully, and differently than we might expect. God gives Joseph a dream that triggers events which eventually position him to play a key role in the rescuing of nations—including his own family. But the key word is "eventually."

Living with "Eventually"

We all live with the not-so-easy condition called *eventually*. And that's why the delay in our destiny, the eventuality of what will be, creates such an important opportunity for us. "Eventually" is a word that inspires both hope and despair. It's the idea that something great is going to happen, that our longings and prayers will, in fact, become a reality. That he'll finally pop the question, the cure will be discovered, the boss will finally notice us, or our purpose will be realized: these compelling possibilities create an "it's worth the wait" hope in us. On the flip side, the idea of "eventually" can also stir despair and angst because, I mean, what does eventually really mean? How long will I have to wait for the update, opportunity, peace, or purpose? Proverbs 13:2 says this: "Hope deferred makes the heart sick." *Eventually* has no set timeline connected to it. And in general, when it comes to our hopes and fears, promises and purpose, we don't appreciate vague delays.

I want to propose that what happens *to* you in your delay directly connects with what happens *through* you afterwards. Because something always happens in the delay. Here are some of the biggies: Distraction. Detour. Discontentment. Discouragement. Defensiveness. Discernment. Discovery. Dependence. Determination. And finally, Development.

Certainly, as you read through each D-word chapter, many other words, phrases, or experiences will spring to mind. And I know that most won't start with a D. I invite you to process, pray, and ponder what God may be saying to you as you move through this book. The words will be different, but I'm certain the development we experience in our delay will be similar.

Before We Jump In

Over the first five chapters of this book, we'll look at what hinders our formation. In the second half of the book, we'll take five chapters to look at what helps develop our destiny. The story of Joseph will serve as the subtle backdrop, but this is not a biblical commentary, nor is it a theological deep dive. I'm for both and appreciate the need for them, and we'll undoubtedly rediscover some Biblical insights and a few deep truths along the way. But *Delayed Destiny* is really an invitation to keep going when we want to quit and a reminder that God is still working in every season and circumstance, even when we can't see it.

We're introduced to Joseph in Genesis 37. But while his life story starts there, it won't wrap up for another ninety-three years over thirteen chapters, all the way over in Genesis 50. This should probably be our first clue that his story, like ours, will develop slowly and involves several delays. A quick overview of Joseph's life tells us that he lived in the land of Canaan and was the favorite of twelve brothers born to Jacob and Rachel. Because he was the favorite, his brothers hated him. Dreams would play a big role in each pit stop on his route to his royalty-like role in Pharoah's household. His dream would set the stage, but three others would play a critical part in his future position in the palace. The second and third dreams involved his fellow inmates. He'd been locked up after being falsely accused of attacking the wife of Potiphar, his boss. While it wasn't true, it did position him near people who had had access to Pharoah before and would again one day. The final dream belonged to Pharoah himself. God would enable Joseph to interpret it, thus securing his release from prison and a new position in the palace. Each chapter progresses painfully slowly but gives us a front-row seat to the providence of God. Joseph would eventually become the second in command in all of Egypt, and his God-inspired plan would prove to be the answer to an impending famine and the key to reconnection with his family.

Delayed Destiny is really an invitation to keep going when we want to quit and a reminder that God is still working in every season and circumstance, even when we can't see it.

Along the way, his destiny was riddled with delays. We'll look at several things that threatened to delete his destiny then and ours today. The first of our ten D-words that we'll dive into is Distraction.

PART 1

WHAT HINDERS

CHAPTER 1
DISTRACTION

Getting Lost in the Details

The first thing that delays our destiny is distractions. We're all bombarded with potential interruptions and inundated with invitations to focus our attention on everything but what we need to. I've often joked that I have the attention span of a fruit fly merged with a junior high boy. While that's not actually true, it can be discouraging to start something or head in a specific direction only to be distracted along the way. I know I'm not alone. How many times have you started something, significant or even mundane, only to be side-tracked? Of course, there's such a thing as a welcome diversion, but many distractions send us down the wrong mental track and take us far from where we intended to go.

For example, have you ever left one part of your house and arrived in another room only to ask yourself, "Now, what did I come in here for?" Ever opened your phone to respond to a text, only to land on some unrelated app or post? I've often sat down to pray and ended up pondering anything and everything except what I was intially going to pray about. We all have stories of succumbing to situations that kept us from fully focusing on our intended objectives.

Shortly before midnight on December 29, 1972, Eastern Airlines Flight 401 took off from JFK International Airport in New York, with 176 passengers and crew en route to Miami. Some passengers were returning home, while others were heading down to ring in the New Year on the Floridian beaches. As they neared their destination, the usual pre-landing protocols began. After setting these in motion, the pilots noticed that the landing gear indicator light had failed to go on. So, they radioed the tower in Miami and were sent into a holding pattern over the Everglades. Once the holding pattern began, the pilot, co-pilot, and flight engineer attempted troubleshooting the problem. As they assessed various compartments to determine if the landing gear had been deployed, they inadvertently disconnected the autopilot. Distracted by their efforts, they failed to notice the gradual loss of altitude so subtle it would go unnoticed until moments before the plane crash-landed in the Everglades. Of the 176 souls on board that early morning, only 75 would survive the crash. Distraction had devolved into death.

The subtle loss of altitude in our own lives threatens to take us out at times, doesn't it?

Of course, most distractions do not lead to fatalities. However, every distraction does have consequences. The subtle loss of altitude in our own lives threatens to take us out at times, doesn't it? We can easily miss what matters most because of something that isn't of real significance.

What distracts you? Whatever it is, you're not alone. God has been urging us to avoid unnecessary digressions and diversions since time began. I love how Eugene Peterson paraphrases James' writings when he states, "But whoever catches a glimpse of the revealed counsel of God—the free life! —even out of the corner of his eye, and sticks with it, is no distracted scatterbrain but a man or woman of action. That person will find delight and affirmation in the action," (James 1:25 MSG).

Maybe your attempts to focus are being undermined by the concerns of everyday life. Theologian Charles Hummel penned a short but powerful booklet called *The Tyranny of the Urgent*. In it, he states that "our greatest danger is letting the urgent crowd out the important." The ding of an e-mail arriving, the screen illuminating with the most recent breaking news update, or the passing thought that hijacks our attention: all come in a package labeled urgent. The moment they arrive, our immediate thoughts shift toward them – if even for a second –our attention shifts, and we must work to regain our focus. Our ability to navigate the ongoing distractions will determine our growth and, ultimately, our outcomes.

Some distractions can be anticipated. Many mislabeled places, people, and perspectives are rooted in patterns, meaning, if we're paying attention, we can spot them coming a mile away. In any case, distraction is inevitable, and how do we prepare for the inevitable? I'd like to suggest that we decide, *before* we get distracted, to press through whatever threatens to disrupt us. I know this is easier said than done. But we do have the capacity to establish patterns of health and intentionality that will keep us from being side-tracked long-term.

Four Cs to Control Your Thinking

Simply being aware of the wrestling match in our minds is a great start. But what do we do about it? I'd like to propose four ways to control our thoughts:

1. Cuff them. Take them captive, and don't allow them much wiggle room in our minds. Arresting a lie when it's little will keep it from becoming a big-time distraction to our day. Simply recognizing that something is either not true or not worth our attention is a great place to start. A necessary next step I often take is to say to myself, "that's not true." At that moment, I subdue that

thought and put it in its rightful place in my mind.

2. Corral them. This allows for greater space in our thoughts but still establishes some parameters that protect us from having our day(s) ruined by internal dialogue. Some distractions are not bad, but they show up at an inopportune time, and you don't have the emotional or mental bandwidth to address them. These thoughts merit more time and prayerful reflection. One way I corral my thoughts is to jot them down in my phone or on a piece of paper. I sleep with a pad of paper on my nightstand so that I can get them out of my head and into a spot where I can come back to them later. It's important to note that lots of these thoughts are good and worth spending time processing them further. Getting them corralled helps me come back to them later.

3. Categorize them. Different categories get more time and your best energy. Placing a particular value on specific thoughts helps us determine which ones to direct our attention and energy towards. For example, dreams and ideas about my marriage matter much more than a passing thought about what someone said to me in the lobby two weeks ago. Forming strategies for loving your community matters more than what you'll have for dinner next week. Parenting and personal health should take priority over other people's perspectives. Thoughts about the future and faith should be put in a higher priority place in our minds and on our schedules.

Let me suggest 10 categories:

a. Faith and family.

b. Personal and people development.

c. Work and worship.

d. Creativity and innovation.

e. Physical and financial fitness.

What would you add? Undoubtedly, your list will look different than mine. But the biggest thing for each of us is to operate on purpose, for a purpose. Otherwise, our thoughts and ultimately our actions succumb to the tyranny of the urgent.

4. Consider them. It's important to take an honest look at the content and quantity that we're allowing into our minds. Considering what feeds and fuels our thinking is critical. A simple question we can ask is, "Am I getting truth or lies planted in my mind?" To consider the content is to ponder what we ponder. It takes but a moment to make an honest assessment of what we're putting in to invite the Spirit to help us apply the other three C's.

> **But the biggest thing for each of us is to operate on purpose, for a purpose.**

One bonus "C" we can apply to control our thinking is putting into practice the words of Peter, who invites us to lean into the greatest resource at our disposal when he writes, "Cast our cares upon him because he cares for us," (1 Peter 5:7). I don't know about you, but I will occasionally cast my cares on him only to take them back later. Jesus wants to carry us and our cares.

Take a moment to insert your Top-10 Categories to Contemplate:

1 _____   6 _____

2 _____   7 _____

3 _____   8 _____

4 _____   9 _____

5 _____   10 _____

Sometimes, my thoughts are pressing but not a legitimate priority. Four years into Newhope's 5-in-5 vision, we had launched four campuses. It was the best of times for our church and the worst of times internally for me. I was having trouble sleeping. More specifically, I had trouble going back to sleep when I woke up most nights. I was waking up distracted. My mind was racing with things to do, conversations to have, disappointments that stung, and projects yet to be completed. Once I finally got back to sleep, I would wake up just a few hours later unrested and unsettled. Something had to change. Rest is a weapon that must be leveraged and fought for. I was missing this critical resource while being ravaged by mental distractions. So, I began to apply the Four C's to my fitful sleeping patterns, and things began to shift for the better. Casting could be another C applied to each category. That verse is a welcome invitation from God to move distractions into prayer moments. The mind governed by the flesh is death, but the mind governed by the Spirit is life and peace. Romans 8:6

Spending unnecessary emotional energy on them keeps me from accomplishing what actually matters. Too many of these distractions and i find myself physically but not emotionally present. But if we can cuff these unplanned thoughts, corral them off from what matters, and categorize them in a way that makes them manageable, we can remain fully present, fully attuned to the tasks at hand. I know well that this is usually easier said than done. But as we continue to practice taking control of what goes on between our ears before it takes control of us, we walk and work with greater effectiveness and ease.

The apostle Paul gave us a great filter when he wrote, "Finally, brothers, whatever is true, noble, right, pure, lovely, and admirable—if anything is excellent or praiseworthy—think about such things," (Phil. 4:8). It can seem nearly impossible to focus our thoughts when we're inundated by so much outside stimuli. However, even in this critical area, the slow-motion-is-still-motion axiom rings true. We slowly but surely begin to cuff, coral, and categorize our thoughts.

Taking Every Thought Captive

When my parents celebrated their 50th wedding anniversary several years ago, I asked my father if he had any insights to pass along to me and my boys as husbands. He pondered the question for a bit and then responded by saying, "Don't say everything you think." That's a great insight that isn't limited to marriage.

I was in a high-level meeting recently that would set initiatives for church planting across the nation, and after leaving, I found myself thinking back to both what was said and what was not said. Two full days after the meeting, I was distracted by thoughts of what I wish had been highlighted. I don't typically linger on *coulda, woulda, and shoulda*s from conversations, but this one was starting to eat my lunch. It's really easy to have our hearts and minds hijacked when we keep rewinding conversations without the ability to change how they went.

Joseph had lots of things that could become distractions. From the day as a boy when he had his first dream to the day when he was appointed as the number-two guy in all of Egypt, he dealt with distractions. During one of the in-between times, he spent a least 730 days in prison, where he had to decide each day not to quit. More on that later. And while I won't presume to know what was happening in his heart and mind, I do know that the outcome of his life was a direct result of his decision, undoubtedly empowered by the Spirit, not to allow the obvious distractions to keep him from the divine assignment.

Let's just imagine for a moment what some of his distractions could have been. There would be countless inward and outward things to distract. The first obvious one would be the most recent events with Potiphar's wife making the unfounded sexual assault accusations against him that led him to his confinement. More on that later. He was probably struggling to communicate with his fellow inmates, as he didn't speak their native tongue. He was missing the comforts of home, including being the favorite son. In a matter of months, he went from not having to waste a minute worrying about anything, to having to watch his back every moment. Imagine the emotional energy he would spend just to get through the day. He was waking up every morning and going to bed every night wondering who he could trust, whether this was his new painful forever future, and if God had forgotten about him. He probably dreamed more than once that what was happening was really just a dream, only to wake up to discover that he was, in fact, living a nightmare. He was a prisoner, in a foreign land, forgotten by the ones who were supposed to fight for him, and there seemed to be no way out.

What Joseph had in unlimited quantities was time. I've heard friends who've been incarcerated reflect on their experience, saying, "Either you do the time, or the time does you." Time can be an incredible gift or a painful prison. Maybe, like Joseph, you find yourself in the prison of time, distracted by what isn't happening during your delay. Joseph developed a dependence on God in these dark times that would strengthen his resolve, and position him both inwardly and outwardly to be used by God.

So, what do we do? The scriptures empower us with the reminder to "take every thought captive and make them obedient to Christ," (2 Cor. 10:15). Maybe you need to limit how much time you allow yourself to ponder what took place. Even incremental steps toward your preferred mindset will eventually get you where you want to go. Remember, slow motion is still motion. Joseph dealt with significant distractions on his road toward development. He somehow managed to keep from burning what was left of his life to the ground as he made his way toward Egypt's second in command. It's

Maybe your best next step is to invite the Holy Spirit to help you pivot from thinking about what distracts to thinking about what develops.

almost always easier to see the favor of God in others' lives than in our own. Like a fish in the water, we can't always see it because we live there. But like Joseph, we have the ability to recognize that God does not waste anything.

Let me remind you now that God is still sovereign over you and is working even in the midst of whatever your distraction looks like today. And though I'm not advocating for a simplistic "just don't think about it" approach (if only things were that simple!), I am inviting you to consider how much time you're spending allowing yourself to be diverted by things that don't matter instead of leaning into this promise and looking for the breadcrumbs that can lead you further toward your destiny.

Three delayed destiny questions when it comes to distractions:

1. What are the predictable distractions in your life?

2. How will you plan for distractions and keep them from derailing you?

3. What have you learned about yourself and God in the midst of your distractions?

Maybe your best next step is to invite the Holy Spirit to help you pivot from thinking about what distracts to thinking about what develops. He'll help you if you invite him. But to get to that place, we must address another thing that threatens to hinder us: detours.

CHAPTER 2
DETOUR

When the Race Goes Wrong: Detours of Our Own Making

Before he ended up in Egypt, Joseph was on assignment from his father to check on his brothers. What seemed like an ordinary day for him would become anything but. In fact, this would be one of those rare days that totally transformed the trajectory of his life. Joseph left the comforts and protection of his parents and headed off to find his brothers. They saw him before he saw them, "and before he reached them, they plotted to kill him. 'Here comes that dreamer!' they said to each other." Normally the designation of being a dreamer is a good thing, but for Joseph and his brothers, it was an insult. They hated him and were plotting his demise. As he approached them, they said among themselves, "Come now, let's kill him and throw him into one of these cisterns and say that a ferocious animal devoured him. Then we'll see what comes of his dreams" (Gen. 37:18-20). And you thought your family dynamics were dysfunctional.

Some detours are of our own making. Others are set in motion by people close to us, like Joseph. Though they didn't follow through on their threat to kill him, they did, in fact, throw him into a cistern. But not until after they'd beaten him. The people whom we most expect to protect and care for us often become the ones who hurt us most deeply.

We've probably all sat down at some point and crafted a bucket list or made some life goals. When I turned 30, I set some "in the next decade" goals. One of them was a physical goal to complete 20 triathlons before I turned 40. Now, a couple of my friends were doing the big daddy triathlons called Iron Mans, which involves a 1.5-mile swim, a 120-mile bike ride, and a full marathon. Much respect and awe for them, but I wasn't doing that. Mine was called Sprint Tris. Essentially, the distances are short enough that, in theory, participants can go full-out the whole race. A half-mile swim, 15- to 25-mile bike ride, and 5k run aren't such big distances that you have to pace yourself (again, in theory).

The first triathlon took place on September 14, 2003, in Kirkland. If you've never been to western Washington, it's quite hilly, with both rolling and steep hills. A few things took place during that first tri that could easily have kept me from finishing. I have asthma, and at the time, even though I had been training, my asthma was triggered by the exertion. So, as I got my bike and the rest of my gear set in the staging area, I put on my wetsuit and reached into my bag for my inhaler. It wasn't there. I was already nervous about what I was about to do, and realizing that I'd forgotten my inhaler at home was not a great way to start the day. Still, I walked over to join my category, the men's 30- to 40-year-olds, at the water's edge.

Our wave wore light blue swim caps. In the wave before, the men's 20- to 30-year-olds, wore white, and in the wave after, the women's 20- to 30-year-olds wore pink caps. As I looked around at my fellow competitors, I noticed something I had failed to see before. Everyone else standing ankle-deep in the lake was wearing swimming goggles. I had forgotten both my inhaler and my goggles. *You've got to be kidding me!* I thought. I'm not usually so scattered. But there I was, and it was now too late to find another pair. This was a moment of decision for me. These seemingly significant items, now forgotten, forced me to navigate some detours of my own making.

Open-water swimming with 50 other guys would be nothing like the training I'd done in the pool leading up to the event. Sure, the ladies in the Senior Aquatic Jazzercize class would get unruly at times, but generally, no one was climbing over me, fighting for space to swim. Before now, my biggest challenge was having one of the senior ladies' water noodles float into my lane. As I stood there contemplating my options, I decided that I'd come too far, prepared too much, and had family and friends cheering too loudly to back out now. So as the air horn sounded, I ran out with the other racers until we got waist-deep in the water and started swimming. With this being my first race, I went out fast. Now, my fast and the other racers' fast were very different. Slowly but surely, several light blue swim caps made their way past me. It turned out that being able to see clearly was important to stay within the race parameters. It would also ensure no wasted time and energy swimming any unnecessary extra distance.

By the way, I mentioned that I had started strong. Really strong, in fact, for me. But not being able to see clearly and begin to wrestle with the labored breathing brought on by my exertion in the cold water was bringing me face to face with a massive detour.

The thing about a detour is not that you don't make it to your intended destination. It's that you don't make it there on the originally intended route or timeline. At a quarter mile, halfway through the swim leg, I was tired, discouraged, and needing a nap—and I still had a quarter mile to go. I turned over onto my back to give my eyes a break and grab a few deep breaths. That's when my nightmare escalated. See, prior to flipping onto my back, I could only see what was going on to my left and right. Now

> **The thing about a detour is not that you don't make it to your intended destination.**

that I had gone onto my back, I had a perfect view of the pink swim caps rapidly approaching. I wasn't super bummed to be passed by the gals— my wife Joanne is a great athlete and had beat me at enough things leading up to that moment that I wasn't bothered by a girl swimming faster. I was bothered that I was moving closer to the middle back of my age group pack. It felt like I was failing in slow motion. I already had to pump myself up to actually step out and attempt this first of 10 triathlons. And now I found myself moving further and further from fulfilling my dream. If I was struggling this much in the very first leg of the very first race, how could I possibly accomplish my goal moving forward? The little voice of doubt in my head began to get louder as each racer passed me.

Someone once asked me why they put the swim portion as the first of the three disciplines, and I told them that you can't drown on a bike or jogging. My detour-filled route through the swim leg had cost me precious energy and time, but I'd survived. Interestingly, when I woke up the morning of that race, I was trying to think and act like someone full of vigor and measured confidence as I approached the race—only to shift from a conqueror's mentality to an *I just hope I can complete this* perspective. A lot of life looks like that. But over time, we recognize detours as normal parts of every journey and begin to lean into them to discover what we can. That's what I did that morning.

One final detour took place while on the bike portion of the race. Let me state clearly that this one was totally my fault. The bike portion consisted of two laps. That's all I had heard leading up to the race. Two laps. The problem was that the two laps were not the same. Each lap consisted of different distances. As I approached the completion of the first lap, I asked a race official this question: "Do I have to do another lap?" That was the wrong question. What I should have asked was, "Do I do the same lap again?" His answer to my original question was technically true. I did have to do another lap. But I needed to do the smaller of the two laps. Unfortunately, I ended up riding three more additional miles than the rest of the racers. Even now, I have a hard time admitting this blunder! What I discovered was that asking the wrong question always leads to the wrong answers.

So, how'd the race finish? Once I got to the running portion, I was tired, irritated at myself, and ready to grab a late breakfast. I'm gonna be honest with you: halfway through the running portion, I thought about quitting. I want to like running, but I don't. In fact, my favorite part of running is when I stop. I was now running beside the posh homes that lined the Kirkland waterfront, approaching a Subway restaurant. I seriously considered popping in for a sandwich, some air conditioning, and a much-needed break. I could rest up and then get back into the race. No one else would know. But I would.

I learned something unexpected but incredibly valuable that day as I crossed the finish line. I wasn't actually competing against the other racers. Even though we were being timed, I was competing against myself. This truth would be transferable to more areas of my life than I could imagine. My marriage wasn't competing against other marriages. Our church wasn't competing against other churches. My finances weren't competing against others' bank accounts. My development wasn't measured against others' development. The lie we're all susceptible to believing is that life is one big competition with everyone around us. I've heard that "comparison is the thief of joy." And I believe it's true. My race, while involving others who were also pushing toward the finish line, could not be run by anyone but me. No one could start or finish for me.

> **The lie we're all susceptible to believe is that life is one big competition with everyone around us.**

Could I have learned these powerful life lessons if I had run the perfect race? I don't know. And what does the perfect race even look like? Each situation provides significant learning opportunities. However, the challenge is to learn what we can from the season we're already in, rather than waiting for a preferred season or setting that isn't here yet. Some of the lessons we learn in the detour seasons of life, marriage, and ministry are the result of decisions we've made, questions we've asked, or places God has put us. All I know is that God never wastes anything. It's what we do during the detour that makes all the difference. Once I discovered that I had taken a detour, I had to determine to keep going, even with my fatigue and discouragement. That resolve to press through the pain and embarrassment allowed me to eventually cross the finish line.

Embracing Flexture: Detours Beyond Our Control

There's a paragraph written to the church in Rome that has been a cherished prayer of mine ever since I first discovered it. Paul writes, "May the God who gives endurance and encouragement give you a spirit of unity among yourselves as you worship Christ Jesus, so that with one heart and one mouth you may glorify the God and Father of our Lord Jesus Christ" (Rom. 15:5-6). Detours require endurance. And a little encouragement goes a long way when we're struggling to finish whatever race we're running. The good news is that God is the one who provides both of those essential elements.

Detours show us that we have the endurance to keep going when we want to quit. Detours, though not preferred, provide encouragement to our spirits because, during the delay, we discover that God has not given up on us, nor is He surprised by the path we're on. Detours display the hand of God. And while we'd most often prefer the familiar to the unexpected digression, sometimes the familiar can cause us to miss the fabulous. Not all detours are bad. New routes and routines expose us to ourselves, others, and perspectives that the familiar can keep us from.

> **And while we'd most often prefer the familiar to the unexpected digression, sometimes the familiar can cause us to miss the fabulous.**

What are you discovering about yourself in your detour? I discovered that I was mentally stronger than I previously thought. I discovered that my goal to complete multiple triathlons would require both physical and mental resolve. I discovered that my preparation for that first triathlon was lacking and that I'd need to train with greater urgency than ever. And I discovered again that my wife's love and support was not connected to my finish time but to her unwavering commitment to me. Where does the Holy Spirit want to lead you? What is He reiterating in your life or ministry while you progress toward the finish line?

Every detour requires a measure of flexibility. Several years ago, we would lead annual mission trips around the globe to partner with the National Church and career missionaries. This particular trip was to South Africa. There were 52 of us heading to Cape Town, to partner with two teams of missionaries. We had a clear ministry strategy that our hosts had crafted. However, despite our well-prayed-through and planned-out objectives, we would quickly discover our need for flexibility.

The school where we were supposed to do assemblies canceled last minute, the kombis we'd rented had been given to another group, and the lodging we'd secured held three to a room instead of four. So, throughout the trip, to both encourage one another and recalibrate us to ever-evolving plans, we'd mouth the made-up word "flexture." Ironically, this principle was never more necessary for me to embrace than near the end of our trip. Two days prior to our departure, we had planned to take the team on a guided jeep safari through a corner of Kruger National Park. This is one of the greatest, if not the greatest, wild game parks in the world. We'd had it on our radar since the early days of planning the trip, having heard from others what a spectacular place it was. We'd even used the safari as a part of our trip recruitment strategy. Needless to say, we were pumped to experience it.

As we finished dinner and wrapped up the reflection and review session from a day of ministry, the missionary pulled me aside and said, "We're not going to go to the park tomorrow." I was confused and initially thought they were kidding. "What?" I said, smiling at them as if to say, "You're joking, right?" But they had decided the day before that they did not want to do the three-hour drive and had made other plans for us. I was beyond frustrated and went, internally at least, into change-their-mind mode. I had drilled into our team that we would honor our hosts, look to them for direction, and trust that they knew what we didn't about living and working in South Africa. And then I didn't want to do any of those things.

I was faced with an inner battle. I know now how silly that sounds. Like I was about to have an adult tantrum. But at the moment, it was like I had been backed into a corner and was ready to come out swinging. Would I throw out the honoring spirit of our trip and fight for my rights as the team leader, or would I trust the missionary and embrace flexture?

Well, just so you know, I've still never been to Kruger. What we did end up doing that day was awesome. We went to a tea farm. I chuckle as I write this because if I'm you, the reader, I wonder how a tea farm could possibly compete with Kruger and actually be "awesome." But it was. It was incredibly beautiful; we had an amazing meal and a breathtaking drive to this oasis. Our stomachs were filled with homemade bread and an amazing chicken dish that was seasoned with something I'd never had before. Not quite curry, and not quite honey glaze, it was the perfect combo of herbs and spices. Honestly, I overate. But the combination of the green tea fields as far as the eye could see, coupled with this once-in-a-lifetime type meal, was a winning combo. We took dozens of pictures. And like always, the camera was incapable of capturing what our eyes were taking in. The tea fields were made up of shades of green that, when touched by the wind, made them appear to be waves on the sea. To this day, participants who I've remained in contact with will occasionally reference what a special day it was.

I am far enough removed and just barely wise enough now to know that what made the day special was not just the beauty of our surroundings and the shared experience with people we'd grown to love. What changed our experience from one of disappointment at our detour to meaningful memories in the moment was our perspective. We had chosen flexture, which provided a perspective that transformed our time together.

It was on that trip that I heard my friend who was hosting us use the abbreviation TIA, which stood for "This Is Africa." It was a reminder that things got done differently there than in my little corner of the United States. We could either be bothered by how and when things transpired or begin to understand that the rules of the game were different. Once we moved closer to accepting (very slowly, I might add) that TIA would impact and often dictate our timeline, we approached every detour with a positive perspective.

In his book *The Doubters' Club*, Preston Ulmer states, "We are formed more by the detours in life than by the predetermined paths others try to set for us."[2] Understanding that our detours are more than mere points of frustration provides the necessary resolve to hang in there and continue trusting the story God is writing. As Joseph waits, stunned and confused in the pit, his brothers decide not to kill him. Instead, they determine to send him on another detour, choosing to sell him to a caravan of Ishmaelites. At that moment, Joseph must have felt a million things you and I have felt in our own lives. He might have gotten angry or despondent; he might have thrown his own temper tantrum. Maybe he felt a little like he was drowning, or felt like giving up the race. But this detour would prove to be the defining moment in Joseph's life, and even the lives of his brothers and father.

Three delayed destiny questions when it comes to detours:

---

2 Preston Ulmer, *The Doubters' Club: Good-Faith Conversations with Skeptics, atheists, and the Spiritually Wounded* (Colorado Springs: NavPress, 2021), 47.

1. What is your initial response to detours?

2. What have you learned from previous detours?

3. What have you learned about yourself and God during
    the detour process?

Viewing our detours through the narrow lens of impatience or exasperation leads to discontentment. And sustained discontentment sucks the life out of each of us. Let's look at the next thing that can hinder the development of our destiny.

CHAPTER 3
DISCONTENTMENT

In Genesis 39, we find Joseph about to begin the next leg of his painful journey. "Now Joseph had been taken down to Egypt. Potiphar, an Egyptian who was one of Pharaoh's officials, the captain of the guard, bought him from the Ishmaelites who had taken him there. The Lord was with Joseph so that he prospered, and he lived in the house of his Egyptian master" (Gen. 39:1-2).

This is the first time we read that the Lord was with Joseph. We don't hear it when he's still at home. We don't hear it when he's beaten by his brothers and thrown into the empty cistern. We don't hear it when it seems like his brothers may spare his life but instead sell him into slavery. It's in the very heart of hurt and betrayal that there seems to be a small ray of hope in Joseph's life. Because God's hand is on him, he has found favor with his new boss. While he'd never have chosen the path he's on, there seems to be a little bit of possibility in his pain. How about you? Can you see any potential in your present pain?

We read in Genesis 39:3-4, "When his master saw that the Lord was with him and that the Lord gave him success in everything he did,

Joseph found favor in his eyes and became his attendant. Potiphar put him in charge of his household, and he entrusted to his care everything he owned. God began to bless the household of Potiphar because Joseph was there." Have you ever paused to think that maybe God has allowed some of the setbacks and situations in your life? Have you ever pondered the possibility that the part you're playing, though essential, is just a small portion of the bigger picture God is painting? Depending on our personality, we sometimes want to be the main character of most stories. Sadly, seeing things exclusively from our own vantage point heightens our susceptibility to scenarios that produce discontentment. Our perspective gets twisted when it's always, or at least often, about us. I can struggle with this at times. Hoping or expecting to be recognized, affirmed, or invited. I wonder if Joseph wrestled with this issue, especially as a young man. Having been designated as the favorite son, he was probably susceptible to assuming that the world revolved around him—at least the world as he knew it.

In my experience, discouragement doesn't start out as discouragement. It often begins with disillusionment. What you anticipated happening doesn't. The people you expected to follow your lead don't. Where you expected to be at this point in your life, you aren't. Disillusionment can easily progress to the point that you are now discontent with almost everything. It's then that the human nature element of wanting to quit when things go bad is at its worst. When there's a delay of any length in what is expected—doubt, disillusionment, and then discouragement creep in. So, what's your leaning? When does discontentment threaten to derail your development? Have you ever thought about what it takes to pull the wind out of your sails? What interferes with your follow-through? If we allow the outward circumstances of life, whether real or perceived, to determine our emotional engagement, we'll lead lives marked by discontentment. Don't pull the

When does discontentment threaten to derail your development?

plug! What is taking place is crucial for your development—as a person, husband, wife, friend, parent, and Christ-follower.

Holding Patterns

There is no quick way to travel cross country. So, when you finally approach your assigned destination, any delay can create some edginess. Unfortunately, sometimes your plane is not cleared to land yet, and the pilot puts you into a holding pattern. I'd never heard the pilot's voice come over the intercom as we descended toward our destination and thought, "I hope he's about to announce an impending holding pattern."

If you're a frequent flyer, you have probably had to "hold" at one time or another. Holding is when an airplane makes several 360° turns to avoid another aircraft or wait for land clearance. As much as every passenger wants to arrive at their destination, sometimes going into a holding pattern is necessary for a safe landing. Holding patterns cause delay, but they also allow for the necessary change of circumstances required for every plane involved. And frankly, delays in air travel are to be expected with all the connecting flights, maintenance, passengers, and weather systems, not to mention the ever-daunting transfer of luggage, which is a whole other conversation. So, let me ask, how are our lives any different? We deal with countless factors on a daily basis that causes delays. Some of these factors are out of our control, while others are very much our own doing.

We will look deeper into this concept in chapter 7, but here are some initial things to consider in the midst of a holding pattern:

- The tower knows what the pilot and passengers don't.

- It's not yet safe to land.

- You have enough fuel to stay aloft.

- Preparation still has to be made on the ground for both safe and timely disembarking.

- Disregarding the tower's instructions has the potential to be fatal, not just for you but for others in the vicinity of your landing.

A delay in our dream's fulfillment should also be expected. We tend to want everything as quickly as possible. We are impatient people. Our demand for a "faster everything" has quickly crept into nearly all aspects of our lives, from food to romance, promotions to riches. Our expectation of getting what we want *right now* has gradually created an unrealistic view of life, love, and learning.

Let's take fitness as an example. Every few months, a new diet or pill is presented as the "get bathing-suit-thin in time for summer" plan. Seriously, do we really believe that what took months or even years of heavy snacking and overindulgence with super-sized fast food, combined with a systematic lack of exercise, will be eliminated from our physiques in just a few short days? The sad answer is yes. We want the shortcut. It's ingrained into us. This lens on life does not make us bad; it makes us human.

> **Our expectation to get what we want right now has gradually created an unrealistic view of life, love, and learning.**

Ever heard the phrase "speed kills"? It's because we weren't designed for speed, but we still crave it. A few years ago, I was in Germany for a business trip. Among the many things Germany is known for, including bratwurst, beer, castles, and countryside, the Autobahn, with its lack of speed limits, is one of its most anticipated. The gentleman I was with owned an Audi A6. This car was designed for speed, and when he asked if I'd like to take the wheel, I didn't hesitate! I'm not a speeder by nature, but when I got behind the wheel, I knew this would be a special moment.

Driving on the Autobahn is like driving on a pool table. It's smooth. The car catapulted forward as I pressed the accelerator closer to the floor. With my back pressed against the seat and my hands clutching the steering wheel, we picked up speed. At 105 miles an hour, it seemed like we were going 50. Then my co-pilot (a career missionary who was part of the 200-mph club) looked at me and said, "Come on, let's go." I pressed down some more. At 130 mph, a jolt adrenaline hit me; at 152, the knot in my stomach was beyond tight. I knew it was time to slowly return to normal speeds.

We are, in general, wired for one of two speeds: fast or slow. And we can easily become disillusioned with God, our boss, our friends, or our family if the speed we prefer is not the speed we're going. To the cautious or those dealing with the discouragement of a delay, let me remind you again that slow motion is still motion.

The 150-mph experience was simultaneously exhilarating and physically draining. At lunch later in the day, I asked our host about accidents on the famous highway. He said, "On the Autobahn, we do not have fender benders. We have fatalities." Unfortunately, in my three decades of ministry, I've seen a lot of wrecks that could have been prevented. There are times when speeding ahead is required, but the frequency of fatalities is greatly reduced when we live a manageable speed. When faced with the disillusionment brought on by a delay, we often want to figure out the fastest way to get out of it. We're impatient people in everything from weight gain to weight loss, downloads to uploads, and finances. Don't pretend you haven't been irritated waiting at your computer or idling in rush hour traffic. Our culture celebrates speed and has grown accustomed to getting what we want right away. But that's not how God designed our development to unfold. Living life in the fast lane rarely produces what it promises and often ends up hurting us and others along the way. Fight the allure of dancing with disillusionment by

> **There are times when speeding ahead is required, but the frequency of fatalities is greatly reduced when we live at a manageable speed.**

knowing that God is working at the pace you're able to respond to.

Three delayed destiny questions when it comes to discontentment:

1. Where has discontentment threatened to derail you?

2. Where have you seen initial feelings of discontentment shift into moments of insight?

3. What have you learned about yourself and God through discontentment?

Joseph was in the middle of a holding pattern. While I'm speculating, the daily disillusionment he must have faced had the potential to be paralyzing. His unknown future coupled with his painful prison sentence must have caused waves of disillusionment to crash over him. You can probably picture the boredom and betrayal that threatened to suck the life out of him. Where has disillusionment crept into your life? What would it look like to lean into your delay and invite the Spirit to develop you there?

The next thing that threatened to hinder Joseph still threatens to delay us now. And that's discouragement.

CHAPTER 4
DISCOURAGEMENT

On Not Giving Up

Discouragement is an equal opportunity offender. Nothing keeps you from navigating this fourth D-word: not your education or appearance, age or nationality, financial position, or love life.

Joseph had a front-row seat to discouragement. He could write a book on the debilitating effects of chronic discouragement. We can often look at pivotal Bible characters and falsely assume that they didn't have similar emotions and responses to setbacks and seasons of heartache as we do. In reality, hopes were dashed; promises were broken. Joseph is minding his own business. In fact, he's thriving in this new assignment leading Potiphar's house. Remember, God is with him. And just when it appears that there is a new chapter being written, he's faced with an uninvited and unwanted proposal: "Now Joseph was well-built and handsome, and after a while, his master's wife took notice of Joseph and said, 'Come to bed with me!'" (Gen. 39:6-7).

It would be hard enough to navigate the trauma of being displaced from his home. Then, just as it looks like some things are going to start going his way, he's faced with another predicament. Don't you know that feeling? The sudden starts and stops we have to face can be incredibly discouraging. Days of peace and productivity can easily be underappreciated until the opposite occurs. You're just minding your own business, stewarding an assignment, and then, seemingly out of nowhere, you're faced with something that knocks you off your feet. For Joseph, this was unwanted advances from his boss's wife, and the ripple effects of rejecting her.

> **Days of peace and productivity can easily be underappreciated until the opposite occurs.**

Joseph chose the right thing when he wrenched himself free from his robe and fled. Potiphar's wife then made some false accusations, and once more, he was on the run, only to be falsely accused of rape and arrested. He was thrown in prison for something he didn't do. But God was working in ways he could never have seen at the moment. The same is true for you. A question we may have to answer is, can someone be walking in favor of God while not experiencing the favor of man? And the painful but accurate answer to this crucial question is yes. God's favor and man's approval often contradict one another.

The Apostle Paul knew a thing or two about discouragement, having faced massive setbacks himself. I mean, if you consider being beaten, shipwrecked, and stoned mere setbacks. (And by stoned I do not mean the "legal in most Western states" kind of stoned.) He would later go on to write nearly two-thirds of the New Testament books. I honestly don't think he'd have been qualified to write as prolifically as he did if he hadn't had to navigate so many setbacks and deal with such constant discouragement.

In one of his letters to the church in Galatia, he writes what I imagine jolted their hearts and ratcheted up their resolve, stating, "Let us not become weary in doing good, for at the proper time we will reap a harvest if we do not give up" (Gal. 6:9). I know that in my life, persistent discouragement makes me want to give up. How about you? Ongoing discouragement can also start to make me wonder if the "good" I'm doing is worth it. Paul reminds us that if we hang in there, even while dealing with discouragement, we'll experience things we could never have if we were to give up.

How many times did Joseph's mind wander regretfully back to that original moment when he decided to share his dream with his brothers? How many days locked in the prison cell did he wonder if his decision to do the right thing with Potiphar's wife was actually causing him harm?

We don't know the answer, but we do know one thing. Joseph didn't give up. The strain of discouragement moves from being debilitating to developing when we, too, make the decision not to give up. I know that can seem like an unappealing idea when we're in the midst of whatever hurts or hinders us, but making that simple decision is hugely significant. Determining that no matter what you face, you're going to hang on, keep fighting, and not give up will strengthen your spirit and mind and steel your inner resolve. Sometimes, we just need to declare, "I won't allow the temporary feelings of discouragement to keep me from the long-term results that resolve will produce." That decision can put a whisper of wind into your sails and set you moving.

> **A question we may have to answer is, can someone be walking in favor of God while not experiencing the favor of man?**

Choosing to Wait Well

Another element that produces pervasive bouts of discouragement is not knowing when things will actually change for the better. It can feel like the breakthrough we're longing for is a receding finish line. We keep running toward it, but it keeps pulling away from us. But knowing when our circumstances will shift is a luxury we don't have. Amid discouragement, we can develop firm confidence that God has not forgotten us and He's actually still working for our good. His pursuit of and provision for us, his creation, is unrelenting. The perpetual nature of His goodness can give us the ray of hope we need as we wrestle with discouragement in any form.

What does discouragement look like in your world? When are the moments where you wonder if you can go on, only to uncover a measure of "maybe I can hold on a little longer"?

Early in ministry, my wife Joanne and I attended a pastors' conference in Southern California, which was where I first heard Pastor Rick Warren speak. I liked him then and I like him now. Of the many chunks of wisdom that were taught, one stood out the most. See, like many of you who attend conferences, pursue mentors, and read books for continued development, we wanted to get the next great tool for growing our skills, the church, or both. That's probably why his words struck me so strongly. Partway through his talk, almost as if it were an afterthought, he said, "You do not determine a person's greatness by their education, appearance, or talents, but by what it takes to discourage them." I think his thought stayed with me because it was so, well, simple. MANY elements help define greatness, but what Pastor Rick was sharing was that much of the things that constitute greatness never come to pass if discouragement derails you.

So, what does it take to discourage you? I don't mean a singular moment where things didn't go exactly how you'd hoped. Those are a regular occurrence for anyone who is attempting hard things. I'm referring to those nagging, won't leave you alone when you're trying to sleep-type situations and seasons that threaten all of our peace. Discouragement threatens to hinder your growth toward greatness. But if you're dealing with discouragement, I want you to know that it's an indicator that you can still feel stuff. Oh, don't get me wrong—I'm not trying to dismiss your discouragement. I just want to remind you that strong feelings and weighty emotions are evidence that your passion and preferences are being tested. The opportunity to fail a test also provides the chance to pass it.

Avoiding Contagious Discouragement

When Joanne and I relocated from Washington to Missouri, we had months of mourning. It wasn't because we felt like we had missed God in our decision or wished we could rewind the hands of time and undo the move. We were mourning what we had let go of. We only knew ministry, married life, parenting, and pastoring in one place. Granted, we're only stewards of seasons, assignments, and dreams. But when you give your life to something or someone and then have to release it, there's often pain. We regularly remind our kids when they're in tough times that it's better to love and hurt than to have no feelings at all. The sadness and sorrow of leaving simply mean that you loved deeply. And I would choose the deep relationships that create heartache over emotionless living every day of the week. With that said, Joanne and I will occasionally laugh and declare to one another, "Hey, it's my day to be discouraged. You'll have to wait until tomorrow." Our objective, whenever possible, is to try not to be discouraged on the same day. That way, we can be a buoy for the other when they're about to sink.

Regularly being around someone who is wrestling with discouragement can rub off on you. Especially for those with strong nurturing gifts. Don't misunderstand me. I'm not advocating that we quarantine ourselves or others when we're dealing with discouragement. I am suggesting that we speak the truth of God's word over ourselves and others while we're feeling the strain of discouragement because there's something significant that God wants to reveal in the midst of it. Here's the principle I'm trying to anchor us to: what gets our attention determines our direction and affection. Whatever you look for is what you'll find. I'm not recommending that we ignore our emotions. But I'm asking us not to stare at what is straining us but rather fix our eyes on Jesus. I'm inviting us to shift our focus off the obstacles and onto the opportunities ahead of us because God has promised that we'll see a harvest if we do not give up.

Jesus' brother James, a key leader in the early church, promotes this life-altering invitation, writing what seems counterintuitive at first glance: "Consider it pure joy, my brothers and sisters, whenever you face trials of many kinds because you know that the testing of your faith produces perseverance. Let perseverance finish its work so that you may be mature and complete, not lacking anything" (James 1:2-4). While we'd never choose trials, they each have the potential to take us somewhere valuable. The pure joy James refers to is not found in the pain of the moment but the discovery of God's presence in the midst of it. Every test is an opportunity to fail. But it's also an opportunity to pass. And as we developed through our discouraging seasons, we began to pass more tests than we failed. And the testing of our faith reveals it to be a building block for our continued growth.

Waiting with Zeal

Discouragement is sneaky. One day we're flying high, and the next day we're trying to keep all sharp objects out of arm's length. Resilience is required for peace to permeate our days. Like many other careers, the ministry provides regular opportunities to practice overcoming obstacles. Will there ever be a time when discouragement stops knocking on our door? I don't think so, because we live in a broken world.

A chunk of scripture that has encouraged and shaped my outlook when I'm navigating a time of discouragement says, "Never be lacking in zeal, but keep your spiritual fervor, serving the Lord. Be joyful in hope, patient in affliction, faithful in prayer" (Rom. 12:11-12). "Never be lacking" could just as easily be stated, "continue passionately doing what you've already committed to."

Zeal is enthusiasm, fervor, and passion. It's not common vernacular in most people's daily lexicon. However, it must be present for us to experience the ultimate objective, which is "serving the Lord." It's not enough to be full of zeal about something. Many people bring a zealot-like approach to their favorite sports teams, political preferences, or coffee orders. I heard about a Star Wars fan years ago who was so committed to being "one of the first to see the premier" that they quit their job managing a restaurant that wouldn't give them the vacation time or sick leave they needed. They were so zealous about Star Wars that they were willing to leave their full-time job to be part of the few who saw the first showing. It seems crazy, but that's how zeal often looks from the outside, and most of us are zealous for or about *something*. The question I want you to ask is, "Is my zeal about my preferences or God's?"

> **Resilience is required for peace to permeate our days.**

Paul provides a three-pronged approach for remaining zealous in our spiritual fervor in Romans 12:11-12. First, be joyful in hope. Hope is a powerful thing. Having hope is medically proven to both bolster and speed up healing. Hope feeds our joy. If I were asked what my top three most valued gifts from God are, I'd put them in this order: grace, love, and hope. Hope is in my top three because it's pregnant with potential that is not based on anything I've done in the past or will do in the future. It's based on a person, Jesus Christ. And his work is done. All we have left is to share the good news and wait for its culminating work. We have unlimited reason for hope, even in our delays.

Secondly, he says we must be patient in affliction. This is the toughest of the three for me. How about you? Ever had someone tell you not to pray for patience or that God would give you a chance to practice it? It's a somewhat comical (if theologically unsound) idea. The point is that we all want patience, but we rarely welcome scenarios that require patience to be applied. Patience provides evidence of the Holy Spirit's presence and power actively at work in us. It's not a valued attribute in our speed-consumed culture. But it's a critical fruit of the spirit needed by everyone. When I'm getting advice from someone during an especially tough time, I will definitely consider the source. And when we look at the life of Paul, with all its highs and lows, we have good reason to take his advice.

Thirdly, we're invited to be faithful in prayer. How would you describe what prayer is to a child? It would probably be a simple definition focusing on God's desire to engage with us regularly. It's a good practice to keep prayer simple, especially when we're struggling. Some of my prayers are really short when I'm wrestling with patience. Other times I could go on forever, airing out my grievances before the Lord. Both are forms of prayer that God welcomes. Faithful prayer looks different for each person; however, the unwavering main character in faithful prayer is an all-knowing, all-loving God.

Now, while these make for a tidy three-point sermon outline, we mustn't separate each of these actions from one another but rather recognize their synergy. The cumulative effect of each produces a complementary outcome. The meat in the middle of these three is our prescription for dealing with discouragement: be joyful in hope, be patient in affliction, and be faithful in prayer.

Three delayed destiny questions when it comes to discouragement:

1.   How can your own wrestling match with discouragement be leveraged to help others pin *their* discouragement?

2.   What has helped you transform your discouraging times into development moments?

3.   What have you learned about yourself and God in the process of working through discouragement?

Our delays are often the result of what is happening around us. However, sometimes, what's happening around us is only an indicator of what's occurring in us. Let's look at our next D-word: defensiveness.

CHAPTER 5
DEFENSIVENESS

Joseph's internal and external battles brought discouragement and delays, which created numerous opportunities to develop defensiveness as his default setting. Trust had been broken, assignments had been taken away, and the dream still hadn't been realized. Each new interaction with others, especially his family and those in authority, could have been laced with a defensive posture. Do you ever deal with defensiveness? Unfortunately, I am not unfamiliar with it.

An ongoing joke at our house involves the phrase, "And no, I'm *NOT* defensive." It's humorous now, but it hurt at first. It was birthed out of an excruciating but necessary season of ministry for me. Sometimes the delay of our destiny is the result of our own defensiveness. I know that's a tough pill to swallow. It's another form of self-sabotage because defensiveness hijacks our capacity to grow. The inability to elicit and receive input, let alone those uninvited critiques that sneak up on us, hamstrings our capability to step into the optimal expression of ourselves. And unfortunately, I had a front-row seat to this in my own ministry journey.

The Mugging

During my fifth year of youth pastoring, I got a call from our senior pastor to come over to his house for a meeting. This was a rare invite. And I don't mean rare in a good way. I affectionately refer to it as "The Mugging." It was July 3rd. I know that because our youth ministry was running seven fireworks stands across the surrounding cities, which we used as a fundraiser and for team building. My pastor had gone to the stand we set up at the church, which was our easiest and safest location. It was also being led by a good guy with no leadership skills. After recruiting and training staff for the six other stands (all required 24-hour security), I was happy to find someone who didn't have a criminal record and had the week of July 4th free. When my pastor showed up at the church fireworks stand to say hello and see how things were going, he realized the guy running things would have been at the very end of any team's bench and only gotten playing time if everyone else was injured or had been ejected. The area around the stand was full of trash. No one greeted him when he walked up. A look of fear which conveyed the thought, "Oh no, Pastor's here to check on us," was what finally welcomed him once his presence on site was discovered. It was obvious that I hadn't prepped this guy the way I should have. So, he asked me to meet him at his house.

When I arrived, there were two other people there. One of them asked me if I would like some water. For some reason, I said, "No, thank you." I would discover just moments later that I'd made the wrong call because I was having difficulty swallowing. My pastor, whom I love and consider a close friend to this day, began by saying, "I have six observations about you; the first one is you're defensive." I really could have used that drink of water then. How do you respond to that? I learned that any way you respond right after someone says "you're defensive" sounds defensive. The other five observations were equally painful.

Regardless, if he was right about any of the six areas, I had to grow. At that moment, I was forced to make a decision. Would I quit, or would I take the steps necessary to develop as a leader, pastor, and person? I began assessing my thinking, planning, and responses to my pastor and our team. I didn't like what I found in some cases, but at least I had a starting point to work from. For example, in my insecurity, I would respond quickly to questions from my bosses about vision and ministry strategies rather than applying what I would later find to be a wisdom-packed phrase: "That's a critical question. Let me think about it for a bit and get back to you on it." Of course, you can't pull out that response in every conversation, but having it in my pocket created just enough margin in my mind to help me process. It was also critical to circle back with them later and initiate my response. Ministry is a privilege. And it also has pain points. The question is whether or not we'll be humble enough to lean into correction and critique even when it's packaged in a way we'd never choose. People have the power to humiliate you, but only you can choose to humble yourself. Throughout that next year, my pastor watched and waited to see if he would fire me or keep me around. It was a tough time. I felt like a puppy with my tail between my legs, peering around the corner, uncertain of my future. Fortunately, he allowed me the months and margin to develop in some areas I needed to address. As I look back on that difficult season, I am truly grateful for it. Now don't get me wrong, I would never have chosen to walk through it. But because of that experience, I set some things in motion in my life and ministry that continues to guide me to this day. I am determined to be a life-long learner, both through formal education and question asking.

> **My pastor, whom I love and consider a close friend to this day, began by saying, "I have six observations about you; the first one is you're defensive."**

The Long Game of Resisting Defensiveness

How you respond when you're facing a forced growth season is dependent upon two main factors: 1) the attitude you bring into it and 2) the voices you listen to in the midst of your mourning. Joseph would never have imagined being betrayed by his brothers and ending up in a foreign prison. Likewise, we will rarely see our forced growth seasons approaching. They can sneak up on us like a right hook out of nowhere.

In Joseph's journey, we get a front-row seat to a forced growth opportunity. He was hurt, deeply wounded, fragile, and dealing with discouragement. But he was simultaneously determined. Rather than allowing the talons of defensiveness to attach to his heart and mind, resulting in the spirit cancer called bitterness, he somehow managed to keep the right attitude.

He refused the right to become resentful. Have you refused your "right" to become defensive?

How we navigate these moments of uncertainty contributes greatly to the development of our faith, character, and leadership skills. So let me ask, does how we respond in one moment determine our destiny? No, of course not. That's too strong a statement. But what about how we repeatedly respond, continuously? What about the patterns we set for ourselves? Those are the things that do, in fact, set our trajectory. My friend Pastor Greg Ford says, "A bad chapter doesn't ruin a good story."

How we navigate these moments of uncertainty contributes greatly to the development of our faith, our character, and our leadership skills.

We've each had some bad chapters, haven't we? How we respond to outside voices, even criticism, will be catalytic for our development.

But our response does not just impact us today, does it? There is a ripple effect. Ever throw a rock into a pond or lake? The initial plop produces a splash, but what follows is amazing. Even the smallest stone thrown into a body of water produces a far-reaching phenomenon! Our daily decisions impact our destiny. We are determining today who we'll become tomorrow. Our daily decisions create a chain reaction in our spirit, resulting in either our development or our slow demise. My friend Pastor Troy Jones says this, "Grow daily, or die gradually."

We were introduced to the words of James, the brother of Jesus earlier. If I'm totally honest, upon initial reading of his words, they seem unrealistic and maybe even unbelievable. But they're not. The invitation to "consider it pure joy whenever we face trials of many kinds" seems like a slap in the face at first. But slowly, as we understand the outcome, our perspective changes. As we humble ourselves, the Holy Spirit continues his transformational work inside us. That's how God always wants to work, producing perseverance in us. Is it painful? Yes. At times embarrassing? Yes. But as I reflect on "The Mugging" and its lessons, I've often said I wouldn't change anything but the lens I used to understand leadership and growth leading into it. God graciously placed someone in my life (my pastor) who cared enough to help reveal my tendency toward defensiveness. An unaddressed tendency threatened to hinder my ability to fulfill my divine design. What's true of me is also true of you—our strengths, left unchecked, become weaknesses. But developed, they have unlimited potential.

Persevering to Joy

You might have asked or been thinking, "How can we possibly consider our pain points as something that brings "pure joy"? I know it sounds crazy! Here's why. If all we see is the test and difficulty in the moment, there's little chance we'll make it to the pure joy perspective on the other side. It's like sitting on a plane at the gate while it's overcast and raining outside. All you can see while on the ground is the obvious. Water dripping down the window. The sun obscured by cloud cover. However, just because you can't tell that the sun is shining doesn't mean it has stopped. Once you take off and slowly make your way to and then through the clouds, you are reminded that there are, in fact, still beautiful blue skies above you all the time. Maybe you needed to read that last sentence today. Like Joseph, everything around you screams that God has either forgotten about you or never cared to begin with. But know that this testing of your faith actually produces something significant: perseverance.

Perseverance, in my opinion, is a highly underrated leadership quality. If we lack depth and determination, we will quit something that's difficult at the first explainable opportunity. In a culture that opts out of most things when they get hard, there is a rich reward for everyone who hangs on.

If we lack depth and determination, we will quit something that's difficult at the first explainable opportunity.

In Joseph's story, we see numerous opportunities where he could quit or, at the very least, choose to carry a spirit of defensiveness. This is evident when he is rejected by his brothers, when he is falsely accused of rape, when his fellow inmates forget him, or, jumping ahead in his story a bit, in how he interacts with his famished brothers when they approach him as second in command. How about you? When faced with scenarios that could either develop you or bring out the defensive warrior in you, what is your default?

At 6'2, I'm the little guy at our house. By that, I mean the shortest of the Portmann men. I remember hearing our youngest son Josiah calling for us from his room down the hall as a fifth-grader. His legs were hurting a bunch, and he was asking us to make it stop. As a parent, I knew what he didn't at the time. What he was feeling were growth pains. We never want our kids to hurt or struggle, yet without that pain, there is no progress toward who they're designed to be. After hearing several moans and that familiar "Mom, Dad, come in here" request,

I went in and sat beside him on his bed. He wanted in that moment what most of us want when we're hurting—for the pain to stop. I proceeded to let him know that if he wanted to get taller, he had to endure this pain. That without the growth pains, there could be no growth. I also assured him that it wouldn't last forever. For him then and many of us in the middle of our painful moments, this doesn't bring much consolation ... even though it's true.

Maybe you're reading this today, and you're in the midst of a painful process that feels anything but worth it. You don't see any progress. There's seemingly no measurable growth in you or your organization. Can I encourage you with this simple reminder? Perseverance produces maturity, even joy. The ongoing development you yearn for is not out of reach.

Because we're never done developing, it can be discouraging if we don't take regular and intentional moments to recognize our improvement. Though forward progress may feel insignificant, slow motion is still motion. An occasional "look how far God has brought me" break will blow wind into our sails and point our thoughts back to God. The sovereign hand of God is the reoccurring thread interwoven throughout Joseph's story. And it's also true of our story. It's easy to miss but hard to forget. Once we develop our ability to discern His hand and presence, even in pain, we begin to experience a closeness to Him that we can't in the easy seasons.

Growing for Good

Another reason to be mindful of the ability of defensiveness to delay and even delete our destiny is that it makes us susceptible to live life through what I call a façade of confidence. Over the months and years, we can move more toward proficiency and confidence in ourselves and our jobs. We can start to feel like *we've got this*. With all we've learned, we can slowly settle into a place of contentment, and I'm not talking about the good kind of contentment. I'm talking about the one where we use the word "contentment," but really, we've drifted into complacency and arrogance. Thinking that we don't need to continue growing is a slippery slope that has significant ramifications for us and anyone who may look to us as a model of teachability.

Proficiency is great, but it can be equally dangerous. My friend Dr. Mike McCrary calls it "the satisfaction of success." This is when we become satisfied with what we've learned or accomplished, only to begin to coast, no longer investing the time and energy necessary to continue developing. We slowly see outcomes that we had only hoped would happen before, and now they've become the norm. We've had success, and it feels good. There's a tension that should be managed here. Success can and must be defined in a way that includes an ongoing commitment to honing our skills and executing our assignments, which means defensiveness must be cut out at the root.

Three delayed destiny questions when it comes to defensiveness are:

1. Where are you susceptible to struggling with defensiveness?

2. What have you done to combat and replace your initial defensive response with one marked by development?

3. What have you learned about yourself and God in the process?

The 5 D's that threaten to hinder our development will never go away. To minimize their effects on our lives is foolish. However, giving them access to our heart, mind, and spirit can be debilitating. How we navigate distractions, detours, discontentment, discouragement, and defensiveness will be pivotal in our ongoing leadership development. They can paralyze or position us for our preferred future. Just remember that slow motion is still motion, and we'll never be done developing. As we shift from what hinders to what helps our development, we start to reach the top of the hill we've been climbing and pick up speed as we move to the downhill part of the book.

Remember, what you do is always the overflow of who you are. Your best shot at significantly impacting society is getting better at what you are already good at. This happens when we lean into direction and correction from those who are further along than us. Our next D-word is often confused with self-awareness, but it's not the same thing. Let's look at the power-packed word: discernment.

PART 2

WHAT HELPS

CHAPTER 6
DISCERNMENT

One of the most meaningful ways the Holy Spirit works in the life of Christ-followers is through discernment. We sometimes think of it as "self-awareness," which is another critical skill to develop. But discernment is different than self-awareness. Rather than you and I being aware of ourselves, discernment is us being aware of the Spirit's promptings.

In Genesis 40, we read, "Pharaoh was angry with his two officials, the chief cupbearer, and the chief baker, and put them in custody in the house of the captain of the guard, in the same prison where Joseph was confined. The captain of the guard assigned them to Joseph, and he attended them" (Gen. 40:3-4).

When I thought about that phrase, "and he attended them," I began to imagine Joseph locked up but still looking for ways to live his life on purpose, for a purpose. So he finds himself with the assignment of assisting these new cellmates. Sometimes serving others while you're in your own cell of confusion sets something in motion you couldn't have orchestrated even if you'd tried.

God often uses people we didn't and wouldn't choose to play roles (often significant, timely roles) in our formation process. What's powerful but not necessarily obvious initially is that Joseph now had proximity to people who had proximity to Pharaoh. Don't overlook the possibility that God has placed some people in your life to help you develop your God-given destiny.

Don't overlook the possibility that God has placed some people in your life to help you develop your God-given destiny.

"After they had been in custody for some time, each of the two men—the cupbearer and the baker of the king of Egypt, who were being held in prison—had a dream the same night, and each dream had a meaning of its own. When Joseph came to them the next morning, he saw that they were dejected" (Gen. 40:5-6).

Joseph noticed the countenance of those he was confined with. When we're in a bad place, whether of our own making or someone else's, it's easy to miss what's happening in others' lives. We can be blinded by our own situation. Discernment's developing power is only unleashed when we're attentive enough to observe it. Joseph took note of the men in prison with him.

Sounds like Jesus, doesn't it? After hearing of his cousin's death, Jesus went to mourn alone, only to be beaten to his destination by a crowd hungry for healing: "When Jesus landed and saw a large crowd, he had compassion on them, because they were like sheep without a shepherd. So he began teaching them many things" (Mark 6:34).

It matters how we handle others when we're struggling. As we develop our discernment muscles, we'll understand that one key to unlocking God's supernatural favor in our lives is helping others unlock his favor in theirs.

In the midst of his confinement, Joseph becomes a confidant to the cupbearer and baker. They would tell him, "We both had dreams, but there is no one to interpret them." Then Joseph said, "Do not interpretations belong to God? Tell me your dreams" (Gen. 40:8). So they both shared their dreams with him.

Discernment is a little sense that makes a big difference. Sometimes it brings the clarity that you should continue, and in other moments, you know to pause. In the "what have you done for me lately" world we live in, the gift and skill of developing discernment is essential, even if defining it is sometimes difficult. That often subtle, occasionally alarming inner prompting makes the green light greener and the red light redder. There are two ways we can go when things get tough in our lives. We can choose to lean in, desiring to discern what God is saying in that season, or we can lean out, pulling away from his voice. When we choose to foster discernment, we're much more apt to hold on when we want to let go. We also begin to understand that God is working in the middle of our mayhem.

It's clear that the Holy Spirit deposited discernment into Joseph's heart and mind as his journey unfolded. While he seemed to operate from a place of discernment-deficit as a teenager, he leads with wisdom after being imprisoned, from recognizing that he could not interpret the dreams to setting a seven-year famine and plenty strategy in motion. Joseph was able to grow. But we all know people who have gone down some rough roads and didn't emerge more discerning at the end of them. As he blew the whistle to start our next set of wind sprints, my high school football coach used to say, "Tough times don't last; tough people do." But just because we go through hard times does not automatically mean we will come out wiser or more discerning in the end. That's something we have to choose over and over again. How do you tune your ear to the Spirit's voice to further hone your discernment?

Discernment is a little sense that makes a big difference.

The Daily Practice of Discernment

Sometimes, we can set things in motion that cause us to forfeit God's favor. Every test involves the potential to fail, but as we've heard, it also creates an opportunity to pass. When Potiphar's wife propositioned him, Joseph was faced with a seemingly no-win situation. Accepting her advances would mean sacrificing his character; rejecting them could (and did) make him the recipient of her ire. There was no easy option that Joseph could take. However, one of them would honor God, and the other would not. And in that way, he was lucky: not every decision we make will be as black and white as his.

Developing discernment is more than a one-time decision to avoid someone or something. We rarely develop anything by avoiding things. While there's great wisdom in evading potential pitfalls, what gets our attention determines our direction. So, focusing on where we want to go more than what we want to avoid sets us on the best road to developing our destiny. For example, if you set a goal to get stronger, you might start by cutting out bad foods, signing up for a gym membership, or getting a trainer. But you can't expect to develop muscles without actually working those muscles. Just going to the gym without exercising doesn't make you stronger—it makes you a creeper. When you get a plan and start to pursue it with passion, you begin to see results. This means living life on purpose, for a purpose. We know that numerous things threaten to hinder our development, but fostering discernment slowly unleashes health and hope in our lives. In his most recent book, *Win the Day*, Mark Batterson lays out, in the brilliant way only he can, the powerful principle of winning every day. Rather than trying to live tomorrow before arriving there, he urges us to tackle today intentionally. He says, "Destiny is not a mystery, destiny is daily habits." The steep hill of growing in discernment that we all have to climb feels way more scalable when we take daily steps toward that objective.

As an adult, I've grown to understand that favor and best outcomes are forfeited when I don't have enough discernment to make the right call. Thankfully, the Bible, and the story of Joseph specifically, offers an ever-growing sense of hope and confidence that the faithfulness of God is far greater than humanity's unfaithfulness. This is where God's providential and sovereign nature tethers us to his foundational truths. He takes broken things and makes them beautiful. We play a part in the story being written; however, God graciously sets in motion and responds to our actions, never wasting anything. So, what does that mean for us?

It's sad but interesting how easily we can lack discernment, even in major life moments. A shocking example of this occurred while Joanne was the assistant manager of a health club outside of Seattle. Because she worked there, I had unlimited access to the fitness center, and one day after my workout, I found myself sitting in a sauna next to an older gentleman. Unprompted, he began to tell me the following story. He started the conversation by saying, "I died at this club a few years ago." Obviously, he had my attention because I knew how the story ended. He didn't stay dead.

He said, "I was running on a treadmill upstairs and suddenly had a heart attack. I dropped to my knees and was shot off the back of the treadmill and died." I responded by asking, "And then what happened?" He said, "Two treadmills over was an EMT who saw the whole thing unfold right before him. He immediately came over and started doing CPR." Someone called 911, and just fifteen minutes later, they arrived to transport him to the hospital. I sat there soaked in sweat, leaning into his every word. He went on to say that he slowly got back into coming to the gym and was feeling fine. When I asked him, "What are you doing differently now that you've had this 'back from the dead' experience?" I expected an enlightening moment with my new second-chance, sage-like friend. His response: "Nothing." Nothing? I've got to be honest; I was disappointed. I was expecting, well, something. Anything that would be inspiring. But he let me know that he was already living his life just how he wanted to, and though he was grateful for the chance to keep living it, he didn't want to change a thing. This guy either had a highly developed sense of discernment or completely lacked it.

Let me ask you the same question. Does it take a near-death experience for you and me to understand the importance of developing discernment? If you got your life back, what would you do differently? Do you have a Spidey sense-type tingle when you answer that question? Would you change anything? Would you shift your thinking, spending, or calendar? How would you spend your time? Who would you fight for? Where would you invest your life? What would you spend your redeemed time thinking about? In his book *Knowledge of The Holy*, A.W. Tozer writes, "What comes into our minds when we think about God is the most important thing about us. God never hurries. There are no deadlines against which he must work. Only to know this is to quiet our spirits and relax our nerves."[3]

Some of us have a Master's degree in impatience, which is ironic when we have access to the Master of the Universe. What we think about God matters. Until we recognize that God is actually for us, working in and through us, we'll miss the greatest resource and relationship available. The Psalmist declares, "Search me, O God, and know my heart; test me and know my anxious thoughts. Point out anything in me that offends you and lead me along the path of everlasting life" (Psalm 139:23-24). Developing discernment means we're open to the Spirit and our friends helping us see anything that "offends" and making the necessary course corrections. It also means living life on purpose, for a purpose. We know numerous things threaten to hinder our development, but fostering discernment positions us to tackle each of them head-on.

---

3 MLA (7th ed.) Tozer, A W. The Knowledge of the Holy: The Attributes of God: Their Meaning in the Christian Life. Harrisburg, Pa: Christian Publications, 1961.

"Are you watching?"

Growing up, our family would vacation in one of two places: the Red Apple Motel in Yakima or the Avenue Motel in Wenatchee. Both cities are in Eastern Washington, where it was always hot. Super-hot. Being part of a middle-class family of five, the quality of the accommodations was never on my radar and didn't really matter to me. What mattered most was whether or not the hotel had a pool, and both did, so we were set. The phrase my parents heard most in those early years was "Mom, Dad, are you watching?" as I attempted various acrobatic entries into the pool.

Back then, I didn't understand the internal need to be seen, noticed, and affirmed. A kid saying, "Are you watching?" or "Mom, watch!" or "Did you see that?" is not unlike every adult who wonders if others appreciate them. There's a longing in each of us to be seen, acknowledged, and valued. From our social media posts and online dating profiles to our résumés, we want to be noticed. Maybe yours wasn't. "Are you watching?" But as kids, we each had some sort of phrase we repeated over and over again as we searched for affirmation and attention. If we're honest, most of us are *still* repeating those phrases. "Do you think I look pretty?" "Did you notice that?" "Have you heard what we're up to here at fill-in-the-blank church?" There is an inherent—and I believe God-given—desire to be noticed by Him, but too often, we substitute God's affirmation for man's approval.

If we're honest, most of us are *still* repeating those phrases.

Still, to this day, sometimes I'll mow the lawn and stand in the driveway, surveying my handiwork, wanting someone else to notice what I just did. Now, Joanne is a very encouraging person and doesn't need me to prompt her toward affirmation. But the moment following my creation of mower lines in our lawn isn't about Joanne. There is something deep inside me, and probably you, that wants to be acknowledged. The burning question we feel inside is this: "Do you see me and what I've done?"

Anyone who has ever created an amazing meal, painted a masterpiece, preached a sermon, or presented a vision knows the feeling of vulnerability that accompanies the moment when what you've worked diligently toward is finally seen and heard by others.

On our final family vacation with both boys living at home, we headed to Joanne's birth state of Hawaii. It's our favorite place to go. And prior to us relocating to the Heartland, we were just a four and-a-half-hour flight from paradise. Once more, the most important thing in determining where we'd stay, even in paradise, was the pools' size and features. And once more, our sons would call across the pool deck, about to dive in, asking, "Are you watching?" Yelling, "Don't miss this!"

A powerful reminder from Proverbs is that as we develop our discernment muscles, we'll discover again and again this reassuring truth: "The eyes of the Lord are everywhere, keeping watch on the wicked and the good (Prov. 15:3). Now sometimes, that can feel like an unwanted tagalong, but only when we're engaged in things that are out of alignment with God's character. But even then, the Bible serves as a draw to dependence on Jesus when we read that God's kindness leads us to repentance (see Rom. 2:4). Because we never outgrow our affinity for affirmation, it's critical to find it in what God says about us.

Joseph had been on his rollercoaster ride of ups and downs when he found himself in prison for a crime he did not commit. He was wondering and waiting. In times of loss, rejection, and victory, we keep wondering and waiting. We keep asking, "Do you still see me? Do you even remember that I'm here?" And throughout the scriptures, we see a pattern of God remembering. Whether it is Noah, Job, Abraham and Sarah, Joseph, Moses, or Ruth in the Old Testament or Lazarus, Peter, or Paul in the New Testament, He does not forget His people. That includes you today.

Three delayed destiny questions when it comes to discernment:

1. Where have you operated with discernment without recognizing it in the moment?

2. What helps or hinders the development of your discernment muscles?

3. What have you learned about yourself and God as you develop discernment?

What does developing discernment look like in your life? In mine, I've tried to have regular POP moments. POP stands for The Power of Pause. A little pause can make all the difference. Creating a little space for grace in our hearts and minds, with our words and actions, sets us up for success. We are poised to hear and discern his voice when we pause and place our trust (back) in God. Developing discernment allows us to remind ourselves who has us in those moments of weakness or strength. And who is always desiring the best for us. "Blessed is the man who trusts in the Lord, and whose hope is in the Lord. For he shall be like a tree planted by the waters, which spread out its roots by the river, and will not fear when heat comes; but its leaf will be green, and will not be anxious in the year of drought, and will not cease from yielding fruit" (Jer. 17:7-8).

The next life-giving outcome in our delayed destiny is discovery. We begin to cross the bridge between discernment and discovery when we recognize delays as steppingstones rather than stumbling blocks. Like a flower that slowly comes into full bloom, discernment ushers us into a place of discovery.

CHAPTER 7

DISCOVERY

Clarity Out of Chaos

When we shift from viewing our delays as problems to viewing them as possibilities, we move into discovery mode. This is when life begins to pack a punch because we understand that even though we get knocked down, we're not knocked out.

When we're sitting on a plane waiting to take off, the cabin begins to get warm. The longer the wait, the more restless the passengers become. They need someone who knows something about the timeline to come on the intercom and bring clarity. A simple "This is your captain speaking. We're experiencing a delay due to a mechanical issue. It's being resolved. We will try to get you outta here as soon as possible. It shouldn't be more than fifteen to twenty minutes. We'll keep you updated." Acknowledging the delay brings clarity, even if what's communicated is not the news we were hoping for.

Here's what I've discovered in my development journey: A little bit of clarity goes a long way. I regularly remind every leadership team I oversee, "Clarity brings confidence, and confusion brings chaos." Chaos in our spirit is so unsettling that it threatens our health and hope. But a little bit of clarity provides a foundation on which we can build.

In chapter three, we introduced the Holding Pattern principle. Let's dive deeper into that concept to see what we can discover:

- The tower knows what the pilot and passengers don't. Our lens on life is always limited. We feel like we have clarity or insight, but if we're honest, we only get a partial view of everything around us. That's not a bad thing and does not indicate weakness on our part. We're just limited by nature. Finite by design. But God is not. God is aware of each and every situation we're in. He's not distant and far off. He's close. This is why tuning our ear to the voice of God—the one in the tower—positions us to develop an attitude of discovery.

  Clarity brings confidence, and confusion brings chaos.

- It's not yet safe to land. If you've ever tried to rush something, whether it's a relationship, vision, or outcome, only to create hurt and heartache, you know the pain of forcing things. At some point, we have to trust that God sees and knows what we don't, and if He has us in a holding pattern, it's for our good.

- You have enough fuel to stay aloft. If you've ever said, "I don't think I can hold on or keep going," only to have kept going, you're reminded that the fuel left in you, though admittedly low, is still enough to continue moving forward. This is why ongoing deposits into our leadership, spiritual, and relational tanks are vital. You can't make a withdrawal of something you've not deposited. You can do hard things. You can withstand tough times. You are an overcomer.

- Preparation still has to be made on the ground for both safe and timely disembarking. Visionary leaders understand the importance of both framework and process. To grow tall, we have to grow wide. Recognizing preparation as an essential part of the process will keep us from forcing things when our expected timeline gets pushed back.

- Disregarding the tower's instructions has the potential to be fatal, not just for you but for others in the vicinity of your landing. Our actions have positive and negative consequences, and taking a broader look at our life and ministry will yield a positive outcome whose impact is not limited to us. One of the first verses I remember putting to memory was, "there is a way that seems right to man, but in the end it leads to death" (Prov. 14:12). Humility puts us in a place where those who see what we don't can benefit us as well. Pride produces pain for us and everyone around us. We get to choose whether we listen only to our own voice or the one in the tower.

Diamonds in the Rough

You've probably heard a couple of things said about diamonds: "Diamonds are a girl's best friend," or "Diamonds are forever." I don't think either is actually true, but enormous value has been placed on these shiny rocks. What makes a diamond so special? Well, for starters, our eyes are drawn to anything sparkly, and diamonds are nothing if not sparkly. They are also nearly indestructible, but a diamond doesn't start out that way. Simply put, diamond formation occurs when carbon deposits deep within the earth (approximately 90 to 125 miles below the surface) are subject to high temperatures and high pressure.[4] That pressure is 50,000 times the earth's atmospheric pressure, and the temperatures reach up to 2500° Fahrenheit.[5] Now, that's severe.

Some stones take shape in a matter of days or months, while others take multiple thousands of years to materialize. Even in its raw form, a diamond requires refinement and polishing. Refinement almost always involves extreme heat, and polishing means being ground.

The process of diamonds forming is similar to our progress into Christlikeness. What priceless character qualities are just under the surface of our lives, waiting to be discovered? Think about what all the pressure and pain in your life might be producing—and think about what it could be with a little refining and polishing. Developing our divine design is a process that's full of highs and lows. In them, we wrestle with the reality of what already is, contrasted with the hope of what could be. At the moment, it feels like it's anything but worth the pressure and pain, but as we slowly begin to take shape, we discover that the wait has made something wonderful.

Waiting for Something Worth It

Several of our friends are Disney junkies. Though I wouldn't put Joanne and myself in that category, we've made many amazing memories at Disney Parks over the years. Our favorite spot is still the original Disneyland in Anaheim, California. There's something nostalgic about it for us that does the trick. One of the shared experiences for every Disney parkgoer involves something we would never pay for outside the park: lines. And often *long* lines. While there are some tricks of the trade, the Disney experience is inherently fraught with this common experience. To be at Disney is to experience delays.

---

4 How Diamonds are Formed blog https://www.1215diamonds.com/blog/how-are-diamonds-formed/.1215diamonds.com/blog/how-are-diamonds-formed/
5 The Ohio State University, "Formation of Diamonds." https://u.osu.edu/cevasco.3/formation-of-diamonds/.

When I asked my Disney junkie friends why they're so willing to endure the waits and how they feel about the lines, I was struck by their responses. They said, "It's not so bad when you know it's part of the experience." Huh. Now, either you will read that last sentence and think they're crazy, or you'll read it and see the perspective they've gained. The second thing they said was equally insightful: "The look on our kids' faces after they've gotten off of a ride makes the whole thing worth it." Wow. Maybe I'm not a good parent. Their delay was worth it because of the experience of those closest to them.

I will admit it can feel a bit awkward to be in the maze of strangers waiting to board a ride. With each minute that passes, you make your way through the labyrinth, which snakes back and forth, ever closer to the start of the ride. What would prompt someone to spend a lot of money just to endure the heat and humidity, huge crowds and long lines? The easiest answer is the experience they have. And when the experience is shared with family and friends, it heightens the joy they feel.

One of the best parts of vacation is the anticipation leading up to it. Having something to look forward to is powerful. It doesn't matter that you know there will be a long road trip or potential flight delays and that even when you finally arrive, you still have to get your bags, schlep them to the rental car shuttle, and wait in another line. The expectation is part of the experience until, finally, you're on your way. What you anticipated made it worth the wait.

> **A delay doesn't indicate disinterest on God's part.**

Here's something life-giving that I've discovered. A delay doesn't indicate disinterest on God's part. He didn't forget about us. He never will. He's working. A worship song familiar to many of us, called "Way Maker," declares, "Even when I don't see it, you're working, even when I don't feel it, you're working. You never stop, you never stop working, you never stop, you never stop working." And when we're waiting in whatever line-like season, knowing that God is working even when we don't see or feel it brings some much-needed hope. And that hope helps us hold on.

Sometimes, though, there are ways to progress forward that don't involve long lines. I recently came across an article in my news feed entitled, "You Can Pay $30,000 To Go Through A Secret Door at Disney World."[6] Here's the central quote that stood out to me: "While visiting a Disney theme park is a magical experience for children and adults alike, guests still have to battle against crowds and contend with lengthy queues. However, for those customers who are rich and famous, a more exclusive experience is offered, and it lies behind a secret door. If you have a spare $33,000 lying about, you can join Disney's Club 33, which affords members 'special access and exceptional service.' The initiation fee is 30k, but it also costs an additional $15,000 annually." Now it's safe to assume that most of you reading this book don't have an extra 30K sitting around to invest in an elite access Disney experience, however, cool it may be. But occasionally, someone will open a door for you in a way you never expected.

For Joseph, it took the cupbearer finally remembering him and having the courage to tell Pharaoh that a fellow inmate had interpreted his dream. For our family, it was a youth leader from a summer camp. One August afternoon, after speaking at a summer camp in Florida for some dear friends, we had the afternoon free. The night before, they had surprised our family with some Universal tickets. After we had gotten into the park and walked around for a few minutes, a guy dressed in a Universal Studios employee uniform approached us. "Hey, you're Jeffery Portmann, right?" "Yes, that's me," I said. "What's your name?" He responded, "I'm Carlos, and I was at the summer camp the previous three

---

6 Lydia Veljanovski, "You Can Pay $30,000 To Go Through A Secret Door At Disney World." *Newsweek*, December 10, 2020. https://www.newsweek.com/you-can-pay-30000-go-through-this-secret-door-disney-world-1658119.

nights. I had to leave to come back to work." And then he said something that would totally transform our theme park experience: "I'm one of the managers here. Would you guys like VIP access?" Of course, we said yes, without fully knowing what that would mean for our time there. Then he proceeded to extend to us something that we hadn't experienced before or since: jumping the line. Our normal theme park experience involved waiting an hour or more for each attraction. However, jumping the line meant we would go through a different door and have access to the front without delay. Wow. It was incredible.

We rode some of our favorite rides multiple times. We got to enjoy the park in ways we never had, and maybe even more significantly, we never felt rushed or weary from waiting. We actually found ourselves saying, "I think that's enough rides for one day." It was an extraordinary, totally unique experience. One thing that made it so special was that it was unexpected.

Even the glacial progression of amusement park lines is a subtle reminder that slow motion is still motion, though not at the speed we'd prefer. Most of our development doesn't involve jumping the line. In fact, most involve long delays. And some of those delays are excruciating. But sometimes, on rare occasions, we run into someone who does for us what we can't do for ourselves. That's really a snapshot of the gospel, isn't it? It pushes the fast-forward button on our experiences, exposure, and opportunities.

Most of our development doesn't involve jumping the line.

We got a sneak peek of Joseph getting out of jail a few moments ago, but what was it that put him there in the first place and what can we discover from that? The overarching theme of Joseph's life is the sovereignty of God. As we saw earlier, Joseph had what appeared to be a "jump the line" opportunity as he began working for Potiphar. Instead, it turned out to be anything but. We read about it in Genesis 39: "Now Joseph was well-built and handsome, and after a while his master's wife took notice of Joseph and said, 'Come to bed with me!' But he refused. 'With me in charge,' he told her, 'my master does not concern himself with anything in the house; everything he owns he has entrusted to my care. No one is greater in this house than I am. My master has withheld nothing from me except you because you are his wife. How then could I do such a wicked thing and sin against God?' And though she spoke to Joseph day after day, he refused to go to bed with her or even be with her," (Gen. 39:8-10).

While jumping the line is often a good thing, sometimes some opportunities seem like jumping the line, but some are an invitation to disaster. We discover some things about our character when we're faced with temptation. Joseph refused to allow his character to cave in by acquiescing to the allure of her advances. We all have areas where we're susceptible to the enemy's advances. If you're unaware of your dark side, it's worth the time and energy to ascertain what it is. It's a cautionary tale that's true throughout time. Unaddressed, we're all one bad decision away from kicking over the bucket that holds our credibility, anointing, and platform.

The enemy will use whatever strength or weakness we have to try to trigger a landslide in our character! In error, I might add, we often think that the enemy will only attack us at our point of weakness. While this is true, it's also true that he is keenly aware of our strengths. You may see yourself as a little fish in a big pond. You may even think you're in no real danger of being on Satan's most wanted list, but you're wrong! Friends, let's not let ourselves become deceived into believing that our value in the Kingdom of God is minimal. Because the moment we do so, we've left the door that leads to our character unlocked. We all need to look at ourselves in the mirror and say, "I'm susceptible because of my weakness *and* my strengths."

Joseph was handsome. His outward appearance attracted attention. You would think that after being betrayed by his brothers, sold into slavery, and now given this attention, his interest would be piqued. It's so nice to be noticed. Affirmation from others is an innate desire in all of us. The question we must wrestle with is this: Is the attention I'm receiving honoring God?

The Reservoir of Your Character

The moment Potiphar's wife propositioned Joseph, he had to go to the reservoir of his character to see what he would do. If you've ever seen a reservoir in person, you know about its unique characteristics. The Cascade Mountain range separates the western and eastern parts of Washington State. It's a picturesque drive. As you head out east of Seattle on Interstate 90, you travel into the beautiful Cascade foothills and ultimately over Snoqualmie Pass. Once you crest the summit and are over the pass, there is a catch basin, a massive reservoir called Lake Kachess. Depending on the time of year, the water level changes significantly as a result of rain or from the snowpack melting. In the wet season, the reservoir is nearly full, with only those logs closest to the shoreline visible. Boats travel safely across the lake to fish. In the early fall, while the weather is still warm, people float around lazily on innertubes. It is a truly beautiful place to observe.

When the reservoir of our character is shallow, it exposes those "dead heads" in us that are usually covered.

However, in the dry seasons, when the water level in the reservoir is shallow, hundreds of stumps can be seen. Fallen logs and "dead heads," which are usually imperceptible, are then impossible to miss. In this season, what was once a vacation destination is now incredibly dangerous for any boat that dares to launch onto it. What was just months prior a picturesque spot turns into an eye-sore that transforms the entire area into a temporary wasteland.

Our character is no different. When the reservoir of our character is shallow, it exposes those "dead heads" in us that are usually covered. So what does *shallow* look like in our lives? For some, it's undisciplined living, a departure from the daily disciplines of spiritual formation, or living life at such a frenzied pace we fail to make healthy, godly deposits. Forsaking the sabbath, neglecting rest, and minimizing the need for margin slowly lowers the level of our character. Secret sin is rarely confessed. And while this does not happen all of a sudden, the slow draining of the reservoir of character leads to fast failures. When Potiphar's wife pursued Joseph, he had to draw from the reservoir of his character to determine how he would respond. Don't kid yourself about this: Potiphar's wife was certainly not ugly, at least outwardly! Joseph must have had a sense that he could probably get away with this without anyone finding out. So, what did he do? He refused. He didn't waiver, he didn't entertain, and he didn't linger. He literally spun out of his coat and ran, passing the test of what I call "The Seduction of Secret Sin."

Listen to the response he pulls from the reservoir of his character: "How could I do such a wicked thing and sin against God?" I wonder if he needed to hear himself say it out loud. He didn't have to explain to Potiphar's wife that everything but her had been put into his care. Maybe he needed a quick jolt of courage or conviction, and it took an audible reminder of his position from his own mouth.

Earlier, we read that "though she spoke to Joseph day after day, he refused to go to bed with her OR EVEN BE WITH HER!" (emphasis added). Think about his predicament for a moment. He easily could have let his heart become deceived with lies from the enemy. Lies like: "You're just a slave," "This is the best shot you're going to get at physical affection," and "It may even enhance your position within the kingdom."

Whether it's an unwanted advance or another area of susceptibility, our response in moments like this is directly connected to the development of our character—to the depth of our reservoir. The temporal always attempts to attack the timeless truths of God's word, but we discover Joseph's response is a heart to honor God, even when the temporal might feel really easy, or even really good, for the moment. He deeply understood God's hand upon his life, even in the complicated, difficult place he found himself.

So, here's my question. Do we regularly stop to recognize the hand of God in our lives? Do we ponder the privilege of partnering with God in bringing the gospel to the world? Are we guarding God's grace in your life? Or do we minimize the opportunity? Do we take it for granted? If we fast forward to near the end of Joseph's life, his father Jacob has just died. He brings his body back to Canaan per his wish. Joseph's brothers are afraid that he'll be harsh toward them without their father around, and they take proactive steps to alleviate this. "But," The Scripture says, "Joseph said to them, 'Don't be afraid. Am I in the place of God? You intended to harm me, but God intended it for good to accomplish what is now being done, the saving of many lives. So then, don't be afraid. I will provide for you and your children.' And he reassured them and spoke kindly to them," (Gen. 50:19-21). Joseph could have been angry with his brothers; he could have demanded their respect and gratitude for everything he had done for them. Instead, he pauses and acknowledges God's movements in their lives. Even though you wanted to hurt me, he tells them, God used and is still using that for good to save many lives, including your own.

Even in the aftermath of Potiphar's wife's advances and his ongoing experience with delay, Joseph discovered that his position, despite his predicament, was a gift from God. Desperate situations give us a clarifying view of our dependence upon God! Are we, like Joseph, using those situations to stare down the Seduction of Secret Sin test? Are we relying on the reservoir of our character and remembering the faithfulness of God?

Walking by Faith When the Path Seems Dark

One last amusement park story. While we served as Network Youth Directors for the NW Ministry Network outside of Seattle, WA, Pastor Kevin Geer and I started taking kids' pastors and youth pastors on what we called a Leadership Journey. It consisted of two face-to-face learning days, reading several books together, and a weekend trip to observe multiple ministries in action. We'd visit churches to get an up close, in-person look at how they were living out the mission of making disciples. Most of these trips were to sunny southern California, so we'd usually catch a Dodgers or Angels game one evening and then spend our final day together at an amusement park.

I should preface the rest of the story by stating that the hotel we were staying at on this trip had an incredible breakfast spread that I jumped into with both feet. When we got into the vans that morning, I had overdone it, having eaten an omelet, bacon, sausage, cereal, fruit, and a pastry, topped off with coffee and some OJ. I was overfull. And then we arrived at the amusement park. Kevin is more like a brother than a co-worker. In addition to having fun with the rest of our group, as one of my closest friends, his goal was to cause me great pain.

So, there we are, our entire group safely strapped into our seats on the coaster, waiting for the "shot out of the cannon" signature to start. Zero to barf is what I call it. The sudden twists and turns and ups and downs are exhilarating. The screams and yahoos from your fellow riders create a shared experience like few other things can. And I should say I like roller coasters, but only the ones that go forward. Forward was fun. But then, when the ride seemed to have ended, something terrible occurred. The exact same experience we'd had going forward began to happen but in reverse. We were heading blindly into G-force turns. Backwards. It started deep in my stomach. Then I got a headache. And finally, I understood what was inevitable. I was about to get rid of my breakfast. I made it off the ride, though my legs and brain felt like the scrambled eggs I'd eaten an hour earlier. Then, I beelined for the restroom, and the rest is history.

Here's the point: I was fine, as long as I could see where I was going. I think a lot of us feel this way. As long as we can see what's ahead, we are comfortable and confident in our forward movements. But that's not how much of life works, and as a Christ follower, it's the opposite of living by faith. Maybe you can relate in other areas of marriage and ministry, love and leadership. The Psalmist writes, "Your word is a lamp for my feet, a light for my path" (Psalm 119:105). Interestingly, most lights don't illuminate our entire path, do they? What they do help us see are the steps right in front of us.

I remember camping with my family as a kid. We were staying near the base of Mt. Saint Helens. This was before it erupted on May 18, 1980. We were near Spirit Lake, and it was a late-elementary-aged boy's dream. My twin sister and I would climb trees, hike to streams during the day, and go fishing. We'd roast marshmallows and tell stories around the campfire each evening. And then we'd call it a night and head to the tent. The thing about tent camping is that there's no toilet inside. When nature called, you'd make your way through the pitch darkness until you were an appropriate distance away from everyone else. In preparation for this, my dad placed a flashlight at the tent's entrance. After unzipping the doorway (some of you can hear that distinct zipper sound in your head), I would flip the flashlight on and make my way outside. It was always surprisingly cold, and it was dark. Scary dark. The flashlight helped me safely pass the picnic table to my designated spot. But it didn't turn the night into day. I could only see so far.

Still, what I could see was just what I needed. And I think that's true for you and your situation even now. We can rarely see as far ahead as we'd like to see. But we can see far enough to keep following the Lord's lead. Have you discovered that God has given you just enough clarity to keep going? While we would prefer a spotlight that illuminates our whole path ahead, the Lord knows that we have enough clarity to keep going.

Three delayed destiny questions when it comes to discovery:

1. What keeps you from asking questions and looking at life through a lens of discovery?

2. How can approaching your delays as pregnant with potential for discovery change your attitude, team, or life?

3. What have you learned about yourself and God in the process of discovery?

It's interesting that even our inability to see everywhere and everything we think we need to actually helps to develop our need for God. This brings us to the next D-word, which, when fully experienced, provides unimaginable strength and peace: dependence.

CHAPTER 8
DEPENDENCE

Alone in the Fire

Joseph displayed an ongoing dependence on God. That can seem like an insignificant statement, but it's not. Too often, people only display an attitude of dependence when they're desperate. But when we're determined to live with that quality as a regular part of our daily lives, we unlock something divine: God's guidance in both the good and the bad.

Sharing the prison confines with Joseph were the cupbearer and baker to Pharaoh, both of whom had offended their boss at some point and been arrested. After being locked up for some time, they each had a dream: "When Joseph came to them the next morning after their dreams, he saw that they were dejected. 'So, he asked Pharaoh's officials who were in custody with him in his master's house, 'Why do you look so sad today?' 'We both had dreams,' they answered, 'but there is no one to interpret them.' Then Joseph said to them, 'Do not interpretations belong to God? Tell me your dreams,'" (Gen. 40:6-8).

We might have expected Joseph to offer some beautiful, compelling interpretation to the baker and the cupbearer, but he didn't. Instead, he recognized that it was beyond him to interpret their dreams. He recognized his inability, but God's ability to speak clarity into their confusion. Little did Joseph know that this acknowledgment of dependence on power he didn't have would prove to be part of his get-out-of-jail journey

Dependence isn't weakness, but it can sure seem like it at times. We often want to show our strength and self-sufficiency. We want to display our ability to make things happen, solve the problem, or assert our authority, expecting this to establish our value. But it doesn't. Not like we might hope.

Dependence isn't a weakness, but it can sure seem like it at times.

When our boys were in elementary school, our family moved to a house outside of Seattle in Kent, Washington. It was a corner lot with a big backyard and a rope swing. Over the years, we transformed it into a great place for playing hoops, barbequing, and sitting around a firepit. Each spring and fall, we'd host our boys' small groups from church, and I'd co-lead them with my good friend Tim McConnell. One night, when all the boys had left and Joanne was in the house getting ready for bed, I sat with Justus and Josiah, enamored by the beauty of the fire. Everything that could be thrown in the fire and burned had already been turned to ashes. It was time to call it a night, so I asked our boys a loaded question. "Do you know the fastest way to put this fire out?" At that point, Siah, our youngest, stood up and was about to put it out himself. I told him to zip up and sit down because if he put it out the way he was planning, we'd all be busted when Mom found out. Not to mention, we roasted marshmallows on this firepit.

Once he sat down and we had a good laugh, I reached for the metal fire poker and slowly began to separate the coals from one another. When the coals stayed in close proximity to one another, they expelled heat and produced a collective array of vibrant colors. It's hard to articulate the beauty of this phenomenon, but anyone who has gazed at a fire knows the oranges and yellows, the pink and florescent hues that fire produces. It's mesmerizing. However, the moment I moved the coals apart, something significant happened. The vibrancy diminished, and the heat dissipated. The coal that just seconds before was alive with color and heat now started turning gray. At that moment, the coal stopped operating according to the synergistic purpose for which it was made.

You don't cook a steak over one coal; you can't experience the beauty of fire with a single ember. As significant an illustration as separating the coals was, what stood out most to me that night was what happened when the coals that had been separated were pushed back into the burning pile. In a matter of seconds, the dead pieces sprang back to life again.

It was a visual reminder of what healthy dependence looks like. The coals were not designed to function alone and essentially can't. At least not for long. Much to our chagrin, we're the same.

There's a natural desire in each of us to establish ourselves as capable and strong. If we're not careful, we can begin to find our identity in our actions rather than in who we are in Christ.

The enemy's best weapon is deception, and if we begin to believe the lie that our best performance and greatest fulfillment are found on our own, we'll stop learning to depend on others. And if we're not careful, well begin to think we don't need God.

I'm a Discovery and Nature Channel fan. Whether it's something about our planet, digging for gold, or braving the elements, I'll usually pause to check it out. Periodically, I'll stumble across a special on predators. My favorite ones involve following and filming a pride of lions. What you'll discover is that, when a pride of lions is on the prowl, they don't run into the heart of the herd; they survey the scene looking for the stragglers.

What is it in us that wants to pull away from the pack when things get tough?

They know it's the kudo or antelope who wanders off from the pack that is most susceptible. It's a numbers game. The odds of a successful attack increase greatly when the number of predators outnumbers their prey.

What is it in us that wants to pull away from the pack when things get tough? Jeremy Johnson, the lead pastor of Northpoint Church, where Joanne and I attend, says, "When we want the relationships the least is when we need them the most." What's your default regarding dependence? Are you susceptible to isolating yourself when riding high or when things get rough? Are you like the lost kudo, stumbling alone into the lion's mouth?

Setting Our Clocks by God's Time

Joseph did not know what was happening outside the prison. He was unaware of what God was setting in motion around him, which would not only free him but rescue nations. God was at work, and Joseph must have known that. He must have asked himself, is God dependable? Can I count on him? Do I trust that He has my best in mind? What Joseph believed about these answers determined his dependence on Him. We're no different. What's happening outside your immediate world? Is it possible that God is orchestrating an outcome that is actually better than what you had hoped or prayed for?

God is constantly moving in ways that can cause us to develop a dependency on him. He's our source. He's able to do and be what no one else can. He is the Great I Am. And he has always wanted us to view him as our King. From the Ten Commandments ("Thou shall have no other gods before me" [Deut. 5:7]) to the Israelites wanting a king they could actually touch and see, humanity is involved in an ongoing wrestling match between our spirit and our flesh, between ruling and being ruled. The Israelites wanted an earthly king, just like all the other nations. But God wanted to be enough for them. We know how that ended. Saul was selected as their King because he looked like one. Our culture isn't much different now than it was then, is it? We want someone who looks the part, even though God says, I'm the only one you can always depend on. Where are you trying to replace God with someone or something you can see? Where has God-dependence been exchanged for something else?

I remember sitting in our idling car with my dad as a kid. We were waiting to back out of our driveway to head to church. But we weren't just waiting to go to church. We were waiting for the rest of the passengers to get into the car so that we could leave. I would later learn this was part of marriage. Now, before the mob with pitchforks and torches begins to gather, we should probably admit that in every friendship or marriage, one of the two people is usually ready earlier than the other. One thing I learned pretty quickly was that honking the horn did not speed up the process but often led to extremely quiet moments as we approached the church. I think it's called "the silent treatment."

At our house, we call it initiating launch sequence. And it's true at that point that "Houston, we have a problem." In my experience, most people don't like to be hurried, but they also hate delays. It's this tension that so many of us must learn to live with in life and leadership. Most things take longer than we want, but we don't want others to rush us.

God's timing and my timing are not always in sync. His timing is always perfect, even though it doesn't feel like it when we're in the midst of our most recent holding pattern. The book of Isaiah says, "For my thoughts are not your thoughts, neither are your ways my ways, declares the Lord. For as the heavens are higher than the earth, so are my ways higher than your ways and my thoughts than your thoughts" (Isa. 55:8-9). Another way of saying it is that His ways involve His timing. The Message Bible speaks to God's timing in this way: "Don't overlook the obvious here, friends. With God, one day is as good as a thousand years, a thousand years as a day. God isn't late with his promise as some measure lateness. He is restraining himself on account of you, holding back the End because he doesn't want anyone lost. He's giving everyone space and time to change" (2 Pet. 3:8).

Do you know someone who sets their clocks ahead so that when it looks like they're late, they're actually on time? I've often gotten into a friend's car and, after looking at their dashboard clock, said something like, "Oh man, we're going to be late," only to have them inform me that "Oh no, we're good. The clock is fast." I wonder if many of our interactions with God involve us getting into the passenger seat with Him driving, then looking at the clock of our lives. We think, "I'm running late!" only to have God assure us that He set the clock, and we're actually still on time.

Thanks to the musical *Rent* and maybe the TV show *The Office*, we already know that there are 525,600 minutes in a year. But minutes are made up of seconds. There are 3,600 seconds in every hour, 86,400 in a day, and 31,536,000 in a year. That's a ton! And when we're waiting, those can seem like they're stretching out indefinitely.

Sometimes, though, those feelings of delay are our own fault. Let's talk about the snooze button. I'd like to give the person who invented the snooze button a handshake or high-five. Snooze buttons were essentially created to delay the inevitable. At some point, you'll have to get up, hit the gym, shower, or closet, and get your day going.

What does your alarm sound like? My alarm goes off most mornings, playing one of my favorite songs. It's a worship song that I've listened to for years. I'll admit, I often set it for 6:00 AM, knowing I will sleepily listen to the song at least once. My wife, Joanne, usually gets up an hour before me, works out, and reads the Bible (she's more spiritual, disciplined, fit, and just a better person than I am.) The snooze button provides a bit of a buffer between my slumber and my showering. But if I'm fully honest, I'd admit that on a few occasions I've found myself hitting and re-hitting the snooze button, so that the song plays on, and I find myself in no man's land. I wonder if we too often push the snooze button when it comes to our growth, decision-making, or prayer. The snooze button puts off the eventual. And the eventual will happen whether we like it or not.

Have you landed in a pattern of delay when it comes to dependence on God? Or have you developed the life-giving, opposite-end-of-the-spectrum, starting-with-dependence attitude when it comes to your relationship with God?

Investing in Destiny

Delays are part of life. Sometimes they're a welcomed and unexpected gift. Sometimes they break our hearts. We can't change the fact that delays are a reality and have to be navigated with a plan and purpose. Here's something to contemplate, though: what's your normal response to a delay? Should you use your snooze button more or less?

Sometimes the price tag for our destiny costs so much that we wonder if it's worth it. But what if, instead of "costs," we thought in terms of "investments"? An investment generally yields a return. What we pour in increases, at times even multiplies, expanding the initial investment. Our dreams are investments we make in ourselves or others that have the capacity to impact our lives and often other people's eternities. That's an investment worth making.

When we start to share our dream with others, it will often make them laugh. But what makes them laugh will make you cry. Because the value we place on our dream will always be greater than the value others place on it. We'll fight for our dream when others will shrug. We'll sacrifice for what, to others, seems unnecessary. However, if we believe in our heart that it's what God has asked us to do, that it's what we were designed to bring into the world, we must lean into the burden we feel and bring it from conception to completion.

How do we put the correct price tag on our destiny?

So, how do we put the correct price tag on our destiny? Where can we get an honest valuation? Here are three questions to shape your process and help you determine if it's worth investing in. First, I would suggest we start in our heart. I realize that can sound altruistic or even naïve. But when determining if it's worth investing your blood, sweat, time, and tears in something or someone, you must have a deep conviction that starts in your heart. A declaration I often made in the early years starting Newhope Church was, "God gave us this dream."

Secondly, we should assess if we're the right person to do the thing before us. Could or should someone else be the carrier of this conviction? The answer may be yes to "could" and no to "should." As we look back at the journey of Joseph, from the pit to privilege, prison to the palace, we see that he was uniquely placed by God to speak into Pharaoh's confusion as well as prepare the nation for the upcoming years of plenty and lack. Could God have used someone else? Of course. God can do anything. Should Joseph have assumed God would use someone else? No. He was strategically positioned to shape the outcome. He would never have chosen to be where he was, but while there, he determined to make the most of it by depending on God's sovereignty and might.

Thirdly, keep in mind that sometimes the act of dependence looks a lot like waiting. Are you willing to keep grinding when your preferred future only shows minute measurables? We've kept returning to the truth that slow motion is still motion. But is there a minimum momentum required for us to keep going when we want to give up? Sometimes the cost we've paid and continue to pay forces us to keep deciding over and over not to quit. I believe it's almost always too soon to quit. In a distracted world, it's so easy to begin with conviction but then drift into complacency. In her insightful book *Grit*, Angela Duckworth writes, "Remember that interests must be triggered again and again. Find ways to make that happen. And have patience. The development of interests takes time. Keep asking questions and let the answers to those lead you to more questions." The Apostle Paul says this, "Do not become weary in doing good, for at the proper time you will reap a harvest if you do not give up" (Gal. 6:9).

Three delayed destiny questions when it comes to dependence:

1. Why does dependence sometimes feel like weakness?

2. How would/has a commitment to develop dependence changed your outlook on delays?

3. What have you learned about yourself and God in the process of learning dependence?

I once heard a preacher say, "When you think you're being buried, you're actually being planted." And that truth has fostered a stick-to-it attitude that only further heightens my dependence on God. Even incremental progress is like gas on a fire that reinforces our resolve and helps us live with the next essential d-word: determination.

CHAPTER 9
DETERMINATION

Determination Over Impulse

My junior year of high school, I had a friend in town visiting from Oregon. He had just gotten a new car called an Isuzu Impulse. The name should have been an indicator of what was about to happen. Because, on an impulse, I asked him through the bathroom door as he showered, "Can I take your car for a spin?" He mumbled something that sounded like "yes" through the cascading water and closed door. So, in my boxers and t-shirt, I grabbed his keys, hopped into the driver's seat, and backed out of the driveway. I had just started learning to drive a stick shift. I wasn't good.

I turned right out of our neighborhood, planning to do a quick loop, return to the house, finish getting dressed, and then head off to church. Halfway through the drive, I saw what the car could really do. And it was fast. I finished flying down the straightaway and turned sharply to go up a hill on my loop back. I had to decide just before the top: I could go straight or attempt the hard left turn. I turned left. And as I did, I oversteered and began to spin out. I overcorrected and smashed the front right corner of the car into a 90-foot pine tree. The car immediately stopped moving.

I was stunned. Just six minutes earlier, I was getting ready for church. And now I was standing on the road in my boxers, trying to flag down a car to help me get back home. This was before cell phones, and I was stranded. That six-minute drive left me six thousand dollars in debt. "Six minutes, six thousand dollars," I kept saying to myself. Not one of those six minutes was worth a thousand dollars. Soon, a car graciously stopped to see what was wrong. I can only imagine what they thought, seeing me in the middle of the road, shoeless and in my boxers. Once they knew what was going on, they agreed to drop me off at my house. I was embarrassed. I was mortified. I was responsible. And now, I was the proud owner of an Isuzu Impulse that I had driven for six minutes. This was not what I had expected with my first car.

The initial rush was now ringing with regret. I was on the hook for six thousand dollars, of which I had about $300. So now I'd have to fig-ure out how to pay my debt. My dad gave my friend $1,000 in cash and then graciously agreed to get a loan for the remaining 5k. I would have to work to pay off the loan throughout my junior and senior years. All the money I was planning to save for college went to a car I drove for six minutes. We still went to church, and I kept waiting for my alarm clock to go off, waking me up from a bad dream. It never did.

Throughout my elementary school years, my dad had been a log-ger. I loved it. I'd get up while it was still dark out and go with him to wherever he was working that day. It was hard, dangerous work, but it was exciting. Now, my dad and I would cut wood every Saturday to pay back the loan. We got into an incredible rhythm working together. He'd run the saw, and I'd grab the rounds as they were cut and toss them over toward our truck. There were times that I was a foot from the chainsaw's blade. We couldn't talk. It wouldn't have mattered if we had tried. It was too loud to hear one another. But we developed a familiarity with each other that made talking unnecessary. We would gesture or give a look and understand what the other person was about to do. We were in sync. Each load of wood—called a cord—would sell for around $300. Slowly, I began to chip away at my debt. I would finally pay off my six-minute impulse ride near the end of my senior year.

Of course, given a chance to go back and press rewind on that six-minute decision, I would never have taken the car for a spin. But what I would not want to rewind are the countless hours with my dad, driving to and from the woods. I would never want to replace the experience of working together.

Take a moment to think about some of your missteps, mistakes, and regrets. Determination was required to rebuild relationships and keep working when you wanted to quit. It's mandatory when there's an overwhelming desire to pull the plug on commitments you've made. It will buoy you when life's storms threaten to push you permanently off course.

What I discovered then, and still apply to this day, is that determination is not actually necessary until there's something you have to battle. It's most on display in situations and seasons that require resolve. Most of these moments are weightier than a kid in a car wreck. But for each of us, what feels heavy and hurtful varies depending on our maturity and perspective.

> **What I discovered then, and still apply to this day, is that determination is not actually necessary until there's something you have to battle.**

When reflecting on our previous "accidents," we wouldn't repeat them, given the chance. But if you look closely and reflect honestly, each of them provided a growth opportunity. Paul wrote to the church in Rome, saying, "We know that in all things, God works for the good of those who love him and have been called according to his purpose," (Rom. 8:28). Even more determined than we are to make broken things beautiful, God is unwavering in his desire to guide and guard His children. We saw it throughout Joseph's journey, and if we pause long enough to honestly assess our lives, we'll see the same thing in ours. God is good. He's sovereign. And that's not just true for others. It's true for you.

There's a synergy and ease that God wants us to experience with Him. The kind of closeness that we share with a best friend or spouse. It's where you're in sync, and the complimentary nature of your relationship blesses you and others. You don't have to talk when you're together. You can. But you don't have to.

So, let me ask, what have you wrecked? What part of your life, legacy, faith, or family seems to be totaled? Will you determine to let God rebuild and restore? If you allow Him, He'll do what we can't. It's hard to believe, but He's more determined than you are.

Hitting the Curb

Most parents are more determined for their kids than their kids are for themselves. It's normal. A parent knows what a child doesn't yet. Teaching our boys to ride a bike was fun and simultaneously frustrating (so was teaching them to drive.) Each of our boys' personalities required a different approach. When it came time for Josiah to learn to ride without the training wheels, we positioned ourselves on the top of the slight hill in front of our house. We had a corner lot that overlooked an intersection. Before you retroactively call CPS on me for endangering him, the intersection was deep into our neighborhood and had only one way in and out. Traffic was infrequent. We were ready for the lesson to begin.

As Josiah sat on his bike, he was filled with uncertainty and fear. Sprinkled in with those feelings was the anticipation of joining his brother and the other neighborhood kids in their daily adventures. Like most of us prior to attempting something new and risky, he straddled mixed emotions. Perched at the top of the incline, I stood behind him, holding the back of his bike's seat and speaking affirmation into his ears. Then it was time. I asked him, "Okay buddy, you ready for this?" quickly followed by a "You got this, son!" And we were off.

Now, maybe your experience teaching your kids to ride a bike was or will be different, but with both Justus and Josiah, I remember running behind them as I held onto their bike seat. I stayed with them for as long as I possibly could, running at max speed in an effort to steady them. But on this day, Josiah was going too fast for me to do the awkward bent-over running form any longer, so I let go. It was a moment filled with hope and anxiety. He sped past our house and picked up speed. But it wasn't just speed that he picked up. He also lifted his feet off the pedals. When the pedals could no longer provide him a balancing point, he began to bob back and forth, accelerating toward the intersection. No cars were coming, but he was still going to have to stop somehow.

As he was bobbing and weaving his way toward the neighbor's yard, I was trying to guide his path with my body. Like when you're bowling, and you've let go of the ball but still try to guide it. And just like with a bowling ball, once I let go of his bike, I lost the ability to determine his trajectory. I leaned my body with all my might to guide him to the curb cut leading to the sidewalk, but of course, it didn't work. He missed it, instead driving full speed into the curb. This sent him flying over the handlebars.

As I stood up the road, watching this unfold in slow motion, I kept thinking, "He needs better parents."

He hit the curb at full speed and catapulted headfirst over the handlebars. Now he was lying on the neighbor's lawn. I raced down the hill to lift the bike off him and check for injuries. Fortunately, with me being Norwegian and my wife Samoan, he was made for mayhem and was physically unscathed. I picked him up, wiped away his tears, and told him that we needed to head back up the little hill and try again. He trusted me, so we did.

And then, as if I'd just rewound the entire traumatic experience from moments before, it happened again. We walked back up the incline, looked down at his preferred destination, and attempted to muster enough courage to do it all over. Once more, I stood there holding the back seat of his bike, I spoke inspiration and confidence into him, and then we started down the hill. As we did, he picked up speed, and I let go. And then, just like before, his feet lifted from the pedals, and he began to bob and weave as he sped through the intersection. At this point, I realized I had not taught him to hit the brakes at that speed. Oh, he was great at braking when doing small circles in the garage, but he had no clue what to do at these speeds. I feel like I can relate to that on many levels. Slow turns in a controlled space develop confidence in me. But life can't always be lived in controlled environments, can it?

And now he'd shot across the intersection and was once more heading, mostly, but not enough, toward the cut in the curb. I leaned again, hoping that this time my extreme body language would make a difference, but it didn't. He went headfirst over the handlebars yet again as his front tire hit the curb. Now I ran to him. He was uninjured but done for the day. This whole thing was a failure, right? Technically, yes. However, that's only what it felt like in the moment.

Earlier, in this book's introduction, I asked a few questions. I asked if you've ever felt like you should be further along than you are now. I asked if you ever wondered why things kept progressing at the opposite pace than you'd prefer. And while the answer to both of those questions will be a resounding yes for most of us, there is something that can be developed in us through the process: determination.

Joseph had to develop it. And he'd have to draw on it over and over again. So will you.

If we lack depth and determination, we'll quit something that's difficult at the first excusable opportunity. We'll throw in the towel because we're just not sure we have what it takes to keep going. But as we grab onto grit and decide to develop some depth, we start to live determined lives that shape our destiny.

One last thought on Josiah's bike riding experience. Even though he had crashed twice, he was slowly learning what it took to manage his speed, lean into the turns, and develop the belief that he could, in fact, learn to ride his bike without training wheels.

As it turned out, that fateful day's bike wreck actually began to develop confidence in him. He now knew he could make it down and across the intersection. This was faster and further than he'd ever "ridden" before. And just a few days later, he would begin at the top of the hill once more, speed down it, make it through the intersection, and safely traverse the dip in the curb. His determination and skills merged to move him forward as a young man.

So let me ask you a question. Ever go over the handlebars of life? Joseph had gone spectacularly over the handlebars on several occasions. Undoubtedly, we *all* have in some way. Going over the handlebars is normal at the beginning. While we're learning new skills or attempting something beyond ourselves, it's not uncommon to fall short or even fail altogether. But if we're too careful, the fear of going over the handlebars of life will keep us from even attempting new things. It will keep us from moving close to God's divine design for our lives. In my experience, faith and fear live right next to each other. We must keep choosing to embrace faith when all we see is fear. Joseph's life is a perpetual reminder that navigating uncertainty and rejection also provides us with a platform to develop determination. And that determination will have a ripple effect far beyond what we could imagine.

In my experience, faith and fear live right next to each other.

Joseph had anything but an easy road to his role as second in command in Egypt. But his determination throughout each stage kept him from forfeiting God's favor and ultimately positioned him as the voice of reason and orchestrator of rescuing the nations. It was on their second visit from Canaan to Egypt during the famine that Joseph revealed himself to his brothers. We read, "Then Joseph could no longer control himself before all his attendants, and he cried out, 'Have everyone leave my presence!' So there was no one with Joseph when he made himself known to his brothers" (Gen. 45:1). He had the power and authority to make them suffer as they'd made him suffer all those years ago. But rather than exact revenge, he extended grace. Now, while most of us will never be responsible for something on the scale Joseph was, we are still very much responsible for stewarding our own opportunities and platform. Our determination to develop even in the middle of delays positions us inwardly and outwardly to bring reconciliation and grace into every relationship. And by the way, when we're determined to live at peace with others, we ensure peace with ourselves. God allowed betrayal, rejection, false accusations, and imprisonment to position Joseph where he needed to be. Maybe he's doing something similar to you.

I know this: God never wastes anything.

I know this: God never wastes anything. No hurt or heartache, no victory or success. He desires to be with us in the ups and downs. He walks with us through our struggles. He doesn't give us a "good luck" at the start and then a "let's grab a picture," at the end. He's with us through the struggle.

Though my dad wasn't with me in the car on that fateful Sunday morning, able to keep me from crashing the Impulse, he was present during the growing process that followed. And in the same way, even though I could not keep Josiah from crashing, I was still with him and loved him. God's the same way with us. He's not out there somewhere far off. He's close. He's Emmanuel—God with us. And he also allows us the freedom to fail. He allows us to get close to the dip in the curb but miss it at times, only to bring us back up to the top of the incline and whisper in our ear, "I'm here; you got this."

Three delayed destiny questions when it comes to determination:

1. Where have you wilted when you should have bloomed with determination?

2. When your preferred future seems to be slowly separating from you, how can choosing determination position you for progress?

3. What have you learned about yourself and God in the process of developing determination?

Determination is a decision we make daily, and it isn't actually required in times of ease and comfort. It's required when things are tough and confusing. When what we hoped and prayed for have yet to be realized. It's in these moments that our determination produces something incredible in us. We slowly, but surely, begin to develop. Remember, slow motion is still motion. And now to look at our final d-word: development.

CHAPTER 10
DEVELOPMENT

How'd I Get Here

Have you ever thought, "How'd I get here?" I'm sure Joseph did, both at the beginning of his life and then again at the end. He was Dad's favorite. His coat of many colors was a regular reminder that his parents viewed him differently than his other brothers. And yet, suddenly, he was knocked down from that place of privilege and preference, sold into slavery, and eventually thrown into prison. Years later, against all odds, he's at the top of the Egyptian hierarchy, and those almost-murderous brothers are coming to him for help. "How'd I get here?" indeed.

In my life, there are two kinds of "How'd I get here?" extremes. The first is when I find myself in an experience, relationship, or assignment that seems too good to be true. The job you never even hoped you'd have is yours. The spouse you didn't have the confidence to pray for is at your side. You're free from hurt and heartache. Experiencing the grace and mercy of God through Christ's work on the cross. Enjoying the joy of lifelong friendships. You end up having children who love Jesus and like you. And you start to wonder, how'd I get here? How could the favor of

God cascade over my life like this? This is a position of gratitude that points all the glory to God. You could never earn it. You understand deep inside that you don't deserve it. But you're grateful for it.

The other kinds of "How'd I get here?" reflection takes place when you've drifted from who you want to be. When you've put yourself in a position to move away from your divine design. It's a place of regret and disappointment. You may think to yourself, "Again? I thought I had moved past this. I thought we were in a new season. I thought good things marked my marriage. I thought the family was anchored. I thought my sin tendencies had been transformed. I had a good attitude for so long. I was eating right and working out. I had been so quick to overlook an offense. But here I am now. Man, how'd I get here?"

Moving with the Current

Without being too simplistic, often the answer to the question "How'd I get here?" is the currents you've put yourself in. We're all going somewhere, on purpose or by accident, but even when it feels like we've just landed somewhere incomprehensible, we've probably allowed ourselves to be buoyed along by a particular undertow.

My wife Joanne was born in Hawaii, and it's our favorite place to vacation in the US. We have many incredible memories there, both as a family and just the two of us. For our 25th wedding anniversary, we went to Maui. It was in a heavy season in our lives. We'd both finished advanced degrees, planted Newhope Church, and been going hard for years. We had ten days in paradise. It was just what the doctor ordered. We were staying in Kaanapali, and we'd ask two critical questions each morning. Are we starting the day at the pool or

> **Without being too simplistic, often the answer to the question "How'd I get here?" is the currents you've put yourself in.**

the beach? And where are we having dinner? Those are our vacation questions. Short. Simple. Refreshing. Life-giving.

On one particular morning, we chose the beach. The day before, we'd gone to a local ABC store and bought two inflatable air mattresses. Joanne voluntold me to blow them up. So, after I'd accomplished that feat, we put on sunscreen, grabbed our snacks, and headed down to the beach. I don't know if you've ever tried to climb onto a wet air mattress while wearing sunscreen, but it's not easy. So, I steadied her and pushed her out from the shore, and she was now floating peacefully. After several attempts, I was able to get comfortably settled in, and we paddled out a little bit farther. Once we were ways out, we took in the experience of sun and warm water, tropical breezes, and no agenda.

It was a meaningful moment as we floated there together. And then some waves came and pushed us apart. Being separated was not what we were looking for. We'd come to this island paradise to have shared moments. And as we floated there the oncoming waves threatened to push us apart. In an attempt to keep the together vibe going - i grabbed the side of her air mattress and held on for dear life. We weathered the next set of waves but it was anything but relaxing for me. With each set of waves, I was being yanked to and fro, and the sets kept coming. So, I tried something else. I threw my leg over hers, and we were able to stay together as more waves came our way. But there was one problem—and she let me know we'd have to solve it. She said, "You can't put your leg over top of mine." I was confused. I said, "What do you mean?" I finally figured out a way to allow us to enjoy this peaceful setting and stay together. What's the problem? And then she responded by saying something that makes me laugh years later. Joanne said, "You can't put your leg over top of mine because I'll get a tan line." I quickly hit her with an accurate and insightful response: "You're already brown." (She's of Polynesian descent, with milk chocolate skin year-round.) We laughed together, but she still wasn't convinced, and her leg ended up draped over mine. This strategy did keep us close together despite the waves, and Joanne avoided the dreaded tan line.

We settled into what was one of the most peaceful moments of the entire trip. We just lay there, floating and enjoying the day. No words. No decisions. Just rest. And then, after about fifteen minutes, I heard some music playing on the beach and lifted my head to discover that we were a quarter mile from our resort. We had drifted. We hadn't noticed it as we were relaxing. Because we were laying back, almost asleep, we had not been aware of what was happening.

How'd we get there? The answer was simple: we had drifted because we were in a current. Currents are often imperceptible to the eye but very much felt, like a leaf that's caught in the wind. You can't see the wind, but you can easily observe its effect.

We all are in currents every day. Our daily development is directly connected to the currents where we've put ourselves. Some currents are subtle, but others are extreme. Even reading this book right now is putting you into a current of inquiry, learning, and development.

What are some of the currents we live in? Habits and relationships, attitudes and addictions, convictions and conversations, and daily disciplines produce outcomes in our lives. What's so life-giving about currents is that while one might have the ability to push us toward something hurtful or harmful, other currents will do the opposite.

I opened the book with good and bad news. The bad news was that you'd never be done developing. And that development almost never happens quickly. What you want to see happen in your life, who you'll become, how you'll be utilized to make this world a better place, the legacy your life leaves—none of that will be experienced in a hurry. The currents you're in right now have brought you to this place. This is not your final destination, or even necessarily your most important, but it's where you are now. Undoubtedly, there are some amazing elements that mark this season. However, there are still places to go that will require some resolution and ongoing development. The current keeps moving, and you're not out of the water yet.

Fighting Against the Flow

The Greek footrace was once considered the most difficult and most violent physical exercise known to man. In one race, Addas, the Victor, burst over the finish line and died from exhaustion. When I first read that, I thought, how sad—what a bummer of a way to go. But then I felt God speaking to me, saying, "The really sad thing is to run to the finish line of life without having spent ourselves fully on what we're called to." Correction received, Lord!

A college buddy, Jeff Smith, wrote a song with the line, "I die daily to the things that once held my heart too tight." He sings about the ongoing battle between selfish, fleshly desires and God's way. While the phrase "die to self" is not actually found in scripture, the concept is, of course, inextricably connected to the idea of being born again. Paul tells the Romans that we're dead to sin but alive in Christ (Rom. 6:6). And then he continues the theme writing to the church in Corinth: "If anyone is in Christ, they're a new creation. The old has gone, the new has come" (2 Cor. 5:17). A passive approach to nurturing a new, ever-growing heart for Christ will bring constant wrestling between the old us and the new us. We could tell stories about what a passive pursuit of purity produces. It's a two steps forward, three steps back dance with discouragement. Dying to yourself requires an aggressive rejection of the selfish, physical, and egotistical desires that stoke the fires of our sinful nature.

This can be exhausting, of course. It can be so tempting to let go and "go with the flow." When we do, we give ourselves over to the invitation to "live and let live." To not fight the reality of what's happening. There is a measure of peace in that. But sometimes, we need to fight. Just going with the flow in the wrong current is a surefire way to live a life marked by regret. Jesus offers us a different way, inviting us into a divine exchange when He says, "But seek first his kingdom and his righteousness, and all these things will be given to you as well" (Matt. 6:33). Maybe there's something there. What we seek, the currents we settle into, will propel us toward Christlikeness and life to the full. The "all these things" Jesus refers to are those things we often chase. The stuff that we think we need to find fulfillment, only to discover that Jesus already knows what we need and is not stingy in providing for us.

Jesus always addresses our most important needs, not our most obvious. You may need to read that last sentence again. It's often the most obvious scenarios that get put on the front burner of our thoughts, energies, and prayers. But Jesus is fully aware of both our most obvious and most important needs and will always default to addressing our most important. He knows what we don't.

Jesus always addresses our most important needs, not our most obvious.

He sees what we can't. He's developing us in what feels like a delay in our destiny.

A Space for Grace

In 1967, Charles Hummel wrote an essay called "Tyranny of the Urgent," which I mentioned in my introduction. Interestingly, even back then, he identified the telephone as among the worst offenders against our peace and contributors to our complacency. I've got one of those phones that, when working properly, is like a minicomputer. You probably do too. We get constant e-mails, calendar changes, and, of course, phone calls. It means instant access for us, but that also means instant access to us. The issue, Hummel says, way back in 1967, is not so much a shortage of time as a problem of priorities: "Our greatest danger is letting the urgent crowd out the important."

In the entire world's history, the one guy you'd think would have a good reason to rush didn't. Of course, I'm referring to Jesus Christ. Jesus wasn't even in a hurry when His friend Lazarus died or when His disciples were sure their boat would capsize at any moment. In the Gospels, we see how Jesus balanced the urgent with the important.

The Gospel of Mark tells us, "Very early in the morning, while it was still dark, Jesus got up, left the house and went off to a solitary place, where he prayed. Simon and his companions went to look for him, and when they found him, they exclaimed: "Everyone is looking for you," (Mark 1:35-37). I lost some of you the moment you read the words "Very early in the morning." But what Jesus modeled was intentional engagement with the Father, which included removing himself from the chaos and cares of everyone else's needs. Jesus left that time of solitary prayer with clarity regarding His mission.

Those five words, "everyone is looking for you," can sum up the pressures of professional life, pastoring, and parenting, can't they? Someone is always looking for us, needing us, texting us, waiting on us. If we don't create for ourselves space for grace—moments of margin that pour life back into our souls—we'll eventually operate on empty. This is why development is not a one-time thing but an ongoing endeavor.

This development requires dying. Let me explain. We read in John, "What I'm about to tell you is true. Unless a grain of wheat falls to the ground and dies, it remains only one seed. But if it dies, it produces many seeds," (John 12:24). To develop your dream, your character, and your destiny, there is some dying required. Thinking back to the Old Testament, we see that Joseph's journey started with his life being marked by relative ease and favoritism, only to be fractured by family issues and rejection. He was essentially buried. But when it seemed like he was being buried, he was really being planted. His life was broken and then blessed.

Sometimes it's those dark times that force us to slow down. It's then that we realize these moments are pregnant with God's purpose. Success and failure are both fatal if viewed as final. Success can make us susceptible to the illusion of self-sufficiency. We can believe we are too mature for mentors and stop asking questions. Let me tell you from personal experience that you have to fight against what I call "Resident Expert Disease." If you've had any measure of success in your career, you can be seen, by yourself and others, as the resident expert. In most rooms we walk into, we are—insert air quotes here—"in charge." That makes us the answer, man or woman. Except, the greatest leaders are not merely answer-givers but question-askers.

Thinking Right

Subduing our ungodly, unrealistic, and unnecessary thoughts allow us to live an undistracted life. So much time and emotional energy is spent on thoughts that we have to make sure we're thinking about what God wants us to think about. It's so easy to let our mind take an idea and run with it. That's why Paul wrote to the church in Corinth and told them to "take every thought captive" and make them obedient to Christ, as we discussed in chapter 1 (1 Cor. 10:2). Now, we read a second directive in the letters to the church in Philippi: "Finally, brothers and sisters, whatever is true, whatever is noble, whatever is right, whatever is pure, whatever is lovely, whatever is admirable—if anything is excellent or praiseworthy—think about such things" (Phil. 4:8).

For a few days in high school, I found myself really wrestling with insecurity and jealousy. Trust me, I know this will sound absurd the more you read about why. Joanne and I were in the early days of falling into "like" with each other. She and her brothers had been spending time with another guy I had met but didn't know well, and I was having an internal wrestling match over it because of how much I liked her. The bottom line was that I felt threatened by him. I finally got the courage to ask her about this guy and let her know that I was wondering if she maybe might "like him." I was blinded by my own insecurities and only saw his strengths. That's when Joanne laughed and told me that this other dude was her cousin. Without this important information, my thoughts were emotionally hijacked by the emotional energy spent on "what ifs." Once I knew the truth, however, I realized just how silly my thinking had been.

Here's the thing: insecurity always invites me to be someone I'm not. I'll forever be a cheap imitation of someone else but the truest expression of myself. In the situation with Joanne's cousin, I had wasted three days pondering something that wasn't possible. Each of us has areas in our life that are susceptible to being held hostage by insecurity and inaccurate information. Imagine the freedom that can come when we lift such unnecessary weights from our overburdened brains.

Are you pondering anything that isn't possible? We experience internal angst when we mistake or misinterpret reality. I invite you to take inventory of your mind. Take your thoughts captive before they take hold of you. Things aren't always as they seem. We can miss major moments in life because we're distracted by something or someone, only to eventually discover that we have no reason for alarm. Can you think of a time when you missed a moment because of an internal wrestling match?

Between the ages of fifteen and sixteen, both of our boys became know-it-alls. It was remarkable. At eleven and twelve, they were inquisitive and mostly teachable. But at fifteen, everything changed. It was as if a switch flipped, and now they knew everything. We'd be sitting at the dinner table talking about whatever, and with full conviction, our boys would tell us why developing countries were having trouble with illiteracy (not really, but you get my point). Now in the moment, Joanne and I both knew that they didn't know what they were talking about. Or, at the very least, they didn't know *much* about what they were talking about. It wasn't that they were bad people or had illicit intentions. They were just in the early days of finding their own voice. After a conversation with my parents, a little bit of reflecting back to when I was fifteen reminded me that I had been the same way.

We live in an information-rich environment. Undoubtedly, the most prolific one in history. But information does not produce wisdom or even insight: "Knowledge puffs up, but love builds up," (1 Cor. 8:1). Even having a position of authority doesn't necessarily mean we're wise, just as being older does not automatically mean we're wiser. And above all, God knows what we don't. While that could cause us to feel stupid or less than, it can also bring confidence and peace. There is someone fully committed to your development. And He doesn't take days off.

One-of-a-Kind, Take-Your-Time Development

The inventor of the Polaroid and founder of the Polaroid Corporation, Edwin H. Land, developed the first instant camera as a hobby during World War II. The Model 95 and its associated film went on sale in 1948 at a department store in Boston, where they sold out in minutes. Two elements that made the Polaroid camera such an incredible invention were that 1) the picture was instant, compared to the previously arduous picture-taking and development processes, and 2) every Polaroid picture is an original. It's a one-of-a-kind. The obvious parallel between how God works in our lives, developing us into His image, is powerful. We are all originals, "one of a kind." And because of that, how we develop will be similar but also utterly unique.

At this point in the book, we've established that we don't like to wait. And that truth even applies to pictures. How many of us had parents with undeveloped film cartridges in one of the catch-all kitchen drawers? I did. And then something remarkable happened. The instant camera that had been invented became more mainstream. Not everyone could afford them, but we were amazed once we saw them in action. You'd point, shoot, and then this film would slowly emerge from the camera.

It was instant. Well, as you know, it wasn't actually instant.

Even when the Instant Camera was introduced, we were always trying to figure out how we could hurry up the process. We'd blow on it or shake it. Some people would put it under their arm while others would stuff it under their shirt. But here's the truth: the image "never touches air, so shaking or waving has no effect," Polaroid Co. says on its website. "In fact, shaking or waving can actually damage the image. Rapid movement during development can cause portions of the film to separate prematurely or can cause 'blobs' in the picture."[7]

According to the Polaroid Company, it can actually take 30 days for a Polaroid to fully develop while your image sits there on the table. That seems crazy, but often, so does our own development. It's never instant because most things aren't. The delay is part of the development. With instant film, we can't help the process, but we can hinder it by trying to hurry. Isn't that true of so many other things?

What if, rather than expecting ourselves to grow immediately, we approached it through the lens of progression?

What if we viewed our development in stages? What if, rather than expecting ourselves to grow immediately, we approached it through the lens of progression? What if we viewed the development of our destiny through minutes, days, and months, rather than just moments?

Measuring Our Growth

There are several ways to mark our growth's momentum over time. Two of my personal favorite ways to ensure that I don't miss my development stages from season to season are to invite trusted voices to speak

---

7 https://www.nbcnews.com/id/wbna4286818

into my growth process and to keep some kind of personal record. I'll admit that asking people who know you well to give unfiltered feedback about who you are at the core can cause some anxiety and even heartache. But not doing it will always create more of both. The process requires appropriate vulnerability. When approaching people who can provide honest feedback, it's important to set conversational parameters. What I mean by that is creating some ground rules and removing any ambiguity regarding what you're asking for from them.

I'll talk with Joanne or another close friend and say something like, "I could really use some counsel about something I'm processing." If I need some encouragement, I'll let them know that I need a cheerleader at the moment and am not really looking for a deeply reflective counseling moment. I'm not saying that I'm always in charge of setting the conversation's direction. That would be arrogant and ultimately unhelpful. But when we're initiating with the five friends I'm about to describe, it's useful to set parameters early on. You'll know what you need at that moment, and asking with specificity will maximize the moment. There's an inherent risk when attempting to develop these relationships. However, the risk of rejection is always worth the reward that results.

I think every person needs these five kinds of friends (or five kinds of things from their friends):

1. A Confidant Friend. This person is a steel trap with whom you can be completely honest and unfiltered. This is someone who you don't have to worry will share your secrets with anyone else. They need to be someone going in the same direction in life as you, who holds similar values. We have to select wise confidants and, if you're a follower of Jesus, who share that mutual relationship.

2. A Counselor Friend. While I am 100 percent for professional counseling and highly encourage it, I am not suggesting that this friend has to be a professionally trained counselor. They should be someone who knows you well enough to provide insight and wise counsel based on where you are and where you want to be.

3. A Collaborator Friend. This person will roll with you. No matter what. I do not recommend the movie *The Town*, but I still love the point of one of its lines. Ben Affleck's character, Doug MacRay, walks into a bar and finds Jeremy Renner's character, James Coughlin, sitting at a table. Ben says, "I need your help. I can't tell you what it is, you can never ask me about it later, and we're going to hurt some people." Jeremy responds without hesitation with the epic line, "Whose car we gonna take?" That is what I mean by collaborator. No, not a literal partner in crime, but a friend who is all in and ready to roll when you need them. We all need a "Whose car we gonna take?" friend in our corner.

4. A Cheerleader Friend. I don't know anyone who has ever been too encouraged. But I know a lot of people who wrestle with discouragement. A cheerleader doesn't blow smoke. They just have the ability to highlight wins and growth in our lives that we may have missed. By the way, our culture tends to celebrate home runs, but four-base hits are even better. And we all tend to hit more base hits than home runs. We do ourselves and others a great service when we celebrate big and small victories because we tend to have many more little victories. Proverbs remind us that "a generous man will prosper, he who refreshes others will himself be refreshed" (Prov.

11:25). Proverbs 18:21 is one of our family life verses. It says, "The tongue has the power of life and death, and those who love it will eat its fruit." How we speak life into others produces health and hope in their lives.

5.   A Cussing Friend. Sometimes we just don't have words to express how we're feeling. Now don't get me wrong. I am not encouraging having a potty mouth and would never advocate taking the Lord's name in vain. I hold tightly to Ephesians 4:29, which says, "Do not let any unwholesome talk come out of your mouths, but only what is helpful for building others up according to their needs that it may benefit those who listen." Another life verse is Psalm 19:14: "May the words of our mouth and meditations of our heart be pleasing in your sight, oh Lord, our Rock and our Redeemer." What I mean by a Cussing Friend is that you need to develop the depth of a relationship with a trusted buddy who doesn't need you to preface what you say or figure out how to word your feelings just right. Now, self-control is one of the fruits of the Spirit and will be a gift you give yourself and others, but there are times when some Christian cuss words best describe what's happening on the inside. Psalms is full of expressive, even extreme language that I'd put in the Christian cussing category, and we could all use a friend who can handle us in our most expressive, most extreme moments.

The second way I like to ensure that I don't miss mile markers of growth along the way is to write down personal reflections. I often do so in the form of private prayers. Whether you're a journaler, a bullet pointer, a blogger, or a vlogger, there is value in marking your growth moments in tangible form. Getting your internal thoughts out can be a helpful way to track progress. Whether on paper or in a digital format, expressing what's happening in your life, including the highs and lows, allows you to look back on the development that's taken place over time. As a pastor friend once said, "We measure what matters." We have some pretty real and raw examples of this throughout the book of Psalms. For example, Psalm 88:6-7 says, "You have put me in the lowest pit, in the darkest depths. Your wrath lies heavily on me; you have overwhelmed me with all your waves." And Psalm 130:1-3: "Out of the depths I cry to you, Lord; Lord, hear my voice. Let your ears be attentive to my cry for mercy. If you, Lord, kept a record of sins, Lord, who could stand? But with you there is forgiveness, so that we can, with reverence, serve you. I wait for the Lord, my whole being waits, and in his word I put my hope." Countless other Psalms express daily situations' heartache and hope, pain, and potential. I encourage you to become a Psalmist and don't hold back. God can handle our extremes.

One critical point I'd like to pass on when you're starting this development discipline is to get comfortable with incomplete and unedited versions of your thoughts. Something I wrestle with at times is wanting my first version to be perfect. And the reality is, if we have to process to perfection before putting something on paper, we're missing the value of the discipline. Getting what's inside of us onto the outside sets us up for healthy assessment.

Another example of the power of development is marriage. As of this writing season, Joanne and I have been married for 29 years. I can say without even a slight hesitation that our marriage has gotten better over time. But it has never grown by accident. It can be easy to grow old together, but not actually grow together. Our marriage has and continues to develop because we're willing to invest in it. Marriage is a perfect metaphor for our relationship with God. Both require work, patience, and an ongoing commitment to keep growing. In our most cherished relationships, short of death, there is no finish line. There is no point where we should say, "Okay, that's it, we're done developing." There can be more friendship and forgiveness, service and sacrifice, and intimacy and intentionality with each lap around the track. The tension with any meaningful relationship is that what we aspire to experience requires effort on the part of both participants. And that effort doesn't always reveal its fruitfulness as consistently or quickly as we desire. It's then that we have to make peace with God's pace.

Assumptions

As I mentioned earlier, Joanne once worked the opening shift as a manager of a fitness center. It was literally across the road from the triplex we lived in. This was like a zero-dark-hundred schedule. I've always loved her willingness to do hard things to help our family follow God's call. Because she worked there, I had a free membership and unlimited access to the whole place. Weights, cardio, pool, the basketball court, and racquetball. I had played football, baseball, and basketball in high school and then basketball in college. I'd taken up golf, which is now my favorite sport to play. But when she started working there, I had never played racquetball. It seemed to be a fun sport, and I honestly expected to pick it up quickly. I mean, come on, it's played in a small space, with no out of bounds, and you hit a ball against the wall. What can be hard about that?

So, I began to play regularly, and when I didn't have a friend to play with, I'd wait to fill in a spot. One day, an older man came in, and his regular opponent couldn't make it. So, when he asked if I'd be interested in playing, I said yes. After looking him over for a millisecond, I began feeling sorry for this guy before we even started. Think Santa Claus, because he could have easily played the part. Under a full head of silver hair (which is now my reality, too), he had glasses covered by goggles and a headband to keep it all in place. His shorts were short, and this was before short shorts were cool again. He was wearing the male version of Daisey Dukes (I'll call them Daniel Dukes because so much of his thighs were exposed). His white t-shirt was straining under the pressure of his protruding gut, and he wore not one but two sets of knee-high tube socks. Of the two of us, I was definitely winning the "looks like he knows what he's doing" contest. But that would be the only winning I did that day.

Assuming I was going destroy him, I graciously asked if he wanted to serve first, thinking this would be his only chance. I was wrong. As it turned out, I was the one who didn't get to serve. He whooped me. And not just one time. I was running around the court like I was trying to avoid sniper fire, and he just slowly pivoted in a small area, commandeering the whole space. I had grossly overestimated my skill level and greatly underestimated his. It was a humbling experience. I don't think he broke a sweat, and I was dripping. He was a gracious winner, and I was a defeated loser.

I had a false sense of confidence about my skill level and assumed, because of outward observations, that I would whoop this old man. What I had failed to do up to that point was develop the skills necessary to play this sport at a high level. For the record, I still don't have them. But I've improved drastically. Development is a decision that no one can make for us. And anyone who reads the book to this point has at least a measure of commitment to personal development. So, I finish with this reminder of good news: Slow motion is still motion. And while you're not where you want to be, you're not where you used to be. You're capable of making decisions that will push you past the pain of the moment and into the promise of development. In his book, *Profiles in Courage*, John F. Kennedy wrote, "Some [men] showed courage throughout the whole of their lives; others sailed with the wind until the decisive moment when their conscience, and events, propelled them into the center of the storm."[8] You're at the center of the storm that is your delayed destiny. And it's worth developing.

Three delayed destiny questions when it comes to development:

1. Where have you seen ongoing development in your life? Be specific, and don't just include big growth spirts.

2. In which situation or season do you feel most open to development? And who have played key roles in you becoming who you desire to be?

3. What have you learned about yourself and God in the process of development?

Conclusion

As Joseph reconciles with his past pain and broken relationship with his brothers, he arrives at a place of healthy perspective, stating, "You intended to harm me, but God intended it for good to accomplish what is now being done, the saving of many lives," (Gen. 50:20).

It can feel like the confusion you're coping with, the delay you're dealing with, and the hurt you're healing from will be what most mark your life. But I have good news to share as we approach the conclusion of this book.

In the heat of a moment, we can wonder if things will always be this way. In the midst of a situation, we can wonder if what we've hoped and prayed for will ever actually happen. There can seem to be no next chapter in the high places of success and the low places of pain. But today is not your last chapter; it's just your most recent. In two weeks or twenty years, what you're dealing with at this moment will just be a part of the beautiful story God is writing through your life. That story is epic and expansive. It's both worth the wait and needed by others. Like Joseph,

8 John F. Kennedy, *Profiles in Courage* (New York: Harper and Row, 1961), 20-21.

you have something to offer that will be unique to you and your divine design. The times of delay in your destiny's fulfillment are not wasted moments. They're important parts of the process that produce something powerful: a new you. And whether you find yourself in a season of exponential growth or delayed destiny, you can be rest assured that God is able to put a period where we put a comma and start a whole new chapter in your life.

With a limited lens on life, it's so easy to think that what we see in our immediate reality will be our forever destiny. Except God is working in and through us to develop something and someone incredible. There is always a delay in the development of our destiny, but maybe we are ready to view the delay as a potential rather than a problem. When a delay takes too long, or we fail to observe the growth we want, we consider pulling the e-brake, which stops all forward momentum and can sometimes cause us to go out of control.

Today is not your last chapter, it's just your most recent.

One of my best friends in high school, Alex Hill, drove a 1986 Chevy Chevette. We affectionately referred to it as "The Vet," short for Corvette. If you're not a car person, I can't stress enough the difference between a Chevy Corvette and a Chevy Chevette. One screams wealthy multiple-car owner or mid-life crisis car. And the other mumbles grandma's get-around-town or quilting club car. What Alex had was the grandma's get-around car. The e-brake only worked on occasion. It was essentially useless because who in their right mind, mid-hill, would apply an e-brake that they weren't sure would do its job? Because it failed more than it functioned, we started playing a game while driving. The passenger or driver would suddenly pull the e-brake while the car was in full motion. What made it funny was that, even though we knew the e-brake was faulty, it still made you jump whenever someone pulled it because you weren't sure if this was going to be the time it actually engaged, causing the car to come to a skidding stop or worse.

On one rainy fall afternoon while driving down a steep hill in Poulsbo, Washington with Alex at the wheel and our buddy Jeff Weible in the passenger seat, I reached forward from my backseat position and tugged at the e-brake. Much to our shock, the brake actually did its job. We began to skid in circles, progressing down the hill toward a steep embankment. This quickly turned into a "what the heck was I thinking, we're all about to die moment." JW, as Jeff Weible was affectionately called, began to utter some phrases that I cannot put into writing here. Alex looked at me with an "if we don't die, I'm gonna kill you" expression that was clearly understood, though no words were ever uttered.

Much to our delight, and honestly to our deliverance, what we didn't know, in the washing-machine-like effects of our spins, was that we were heading for a stand of trees near the edge of the embankment that had recently been cut. With one last spin, we came to a complete and sudden stop. Our rear bumper slammed into a stump just ten feet from the drop-off. The trees had been cut, but they hadn't been fully cleared. We were saved. We sat there stunned. A mixture of relief, shock, and laughter overcame us. We weren't going to die. The car's bumper was bent, but we didn't even have a bruise.

The car's bumper was bent, but we didn't even have a bruise.

Maybe you find yourself reading this final thought and feel like you or someone close to you just pulled the e-brake. Maybe your life feels like the Chevette, spinning out of control. Or maybe you've stopped spinning and are sitting in stunned silence. Know this. You might be a little bit bent, but you're not broken.

It's almost always too soon to quit.

You have a delayed destiny.

But it can be developed.

Don't quit.

DELAYED DESTINY DISCUSSION QUESTIONS

Chapter 1, Distractions

1. What are the predictable distractions in your life?

2. How will you plan for distractions and not allow them to derail you?

3. What is God teaching you in the midst of your distractions?

Chapter 2, Detours

1. What is your initial response to detours?

2. What have you learned from previous detours?

3. What have you learned about yourself and God during the detour process?

Chapter 3, Disillusionment

1. Where has disillusionment threatened to derail you?

2. Where have you seen initial feelings of disillusionment shift into moments of insight?

3. What have you learned about yourself and God in the process of disillusionment?

Chapter 4, Discouragement

1. How can your wrestling match with discouragement be leveraged to help others pin their own discouragement?

2. What has helped you transform your discouragement from stumbling blocks to stepping stones?

3. What have you learned about yourself and God in the process of discouragement?

Chapter 5, Defensiveness

1. Where are you susceptible to struggle with defensiveness?

2. What have you done to combat and replace your initial defensive response with one marked by development?

3. What have you learned about yourself and God in the process of defensiveness?

Chapter 6, Discernment

1. Where have you operated with discernment, but didn't recognize it in the moment?

2. What helps or hinders the development of your discernment muscles?

3. What have you learned about yourself and God in the process of discernment?

Chapter 7, Discovery

1. What keeps you from asking questions and looking at life through a lens of discovery?

2. How has approaching your delays as pregnant with potential changed your attitude, team, or life?

3. What have you learned about yourself and God in the process of discovery?

Chapter 8, Dependence

1. Why does dependence feel like weakness at times?

2. How would/has a commitment to develop dependence changed your outlook on delays?

3. What have you learned about yourself and God in the process of dependence?

Chapter 9, Determination

1. Where have you wilted when you should have bloomed with determination?

2. When your preferred future seems to be slowly separating from you, how can choosing determination position you for progress?

3. What have you learned about yourself and God in the process of developing determination?

Chapter 10, Development

1. Where have you wilted when you should have bloomed when it comes to developing determination?

2. Can you look back and see incremental growth? How does that affirm your commitment to ongoing development?

3. What have you learned about yourself and God in the process of development?

DELAYED DESTINY
ADDITIONAL DEEP
DIVE SCRIPTURES

Exodus:

"The Lord is my strength and my defense; he has become my salvation. He is my God, and I will praise him, my father's God, and I will exalt him."

Exodus 15:2

Deuteronomy:

For the Lord your God is the one who goes with you to fight for you against your enemies to give you victory.

Deuteronomy 20:4

Joshua:

"Be strong and very courageous. Be careful to obey all the law my servant Moses gave you; do not turn from it to the right or to the left, that you may be successful wherever you go. Keep this Book of the Law always on your lips; meditate on it day and night, so that you may be careful to do everything written in it. Then you will be prosperous and successful. Have I not commanded you? Be strong and courageous. Do not be afraid; do not be discouraged, for the Lord your God will be with you wherever you go."

Joshua 1:7-9

Nehemiah:

Nehemiah said, "Go and enjoy choice food and sweet drinks, and send some to those who have nothing prepared. This day is holy to our Lord. Do not grieve, for the joy of the Lord is your strength."

Nehemiah 8:10

Psalm:

I love you, Lord, my strength. The Lord is my rock, my fortress and my deliverer; my God is my rock, in whom I take refuge, my shield and the horn of my salvation, my stronghold.

Psalm 18:1-2

The Lord is my shepherd, I lack nothing. He makes me lie down in green pastures, he leads me beside quiet waters, he refreshes my soul. He guides me along the right paths for his name's sake. Even though I walk through the darkest valley, I will fear no evil, for you are with me; your rod and your staff, they comfort me. You prepare a table before me in the presence of my enemies. You anoint my head with oil; my cup overflows. Surely your goodness and love will follow me all the days of my life, and I will dwell in the house of the Lord forever.

Psalm 23:1-8

The Lord is my light and my salvation—whom shall I fear? The Lord is the stronghold of my life—of whom shall I be afraid?

Psalm 27:1

God is our refuge and strength, an ever-present help in trouble.

Psalm 46:1

But I will sing of your strength, in the morning I will sing of your love; for you are my fortress, my refuge in times of trouble.

Psalm 59:16

For you have been my hope, Sovereign Lord, my confidence since my youth. From birth I have relied on you; you brought me forth from my mother's womb. I will ever praise you.

Psalm 71:5-6

My flesh and my heart may fail, but God is the strength of my heart and my portion forever. Those who are far from you will perish; you destroy all who are unfaithful to you. But as for me, it is good to be near God. I have made the Sovereign Lord my refuge; I will tell of all your deeds.

Psalm 73:26

Teach me your way, O Lord, that I may walk in your truth; unite my heart to fear your name.

Psalm 86:11

For he satisfies the longing soul, and the hungry soul he fills with good things.

Psalm 107:9

How can a young person stay on the path of purity? By living according to your word. I seek you with all my heart; do not let me stray from your commands. I have hidden your word in my heart that I might not sin against you.

Psalm 119:9-11

My soul is weary with sorrow; strengthen me according to your unfailing word.

Psalm 119:28

Isaiah:

Surely God is my salvation; I will trust and not be afraid. The Lord, the Lord himself, is my strength and my defense; he has become my salvation."

Isaiah 12:2

Lord, be gracious to us; we long for you. Be our strength every morning, our salvation in time of distress.

Isaiah 33:2

He gives strength to the weary and increases the power of the weak. Even youths grow tired and weary, and young men stumble and fall; but those who hope in the Lord will renew their strength. They will soar on wings like eagles; they will run and not grow weary, they will walk and not be faint.

Isaiah 40:29-31

So do not fear, for I am with you; do not be dismayed, for I am your God. I will strengthen you and help you; I will uphold you with my righteous right hand.

Isaiah 41:10

Lamentations:

The steadfast love of the Lord never ceases; his mercies never come to an end; they are new every morning; great is your faithfulness. "The Lord is my portion," says my soul, "therefore I will have hope in him."

Lamentations 3:22-24

Habakkuk:

The Sovereign Lord is my strength; he makes my feet like the feet of a deer, he enables me to tread on the heights.

Habakkuk 3:19

Matthew:

Because of the increase of wickedness, the love of most will grow cold, 13 but the one who stands firm to the end will be saved.

Matthew 24:12-13

Luke:

For nothing will be impossible with God.

Luke 1:37

"And Jesus grew in wisdom and stature, and in favor with God and man."

Luke 2:52

John:

"All this I have spoken while still with you. But the Advocate, the Holy Spirit, whom the Father will send in my name, will teach you all things and will remind you of everything I have said to you. Peace I leave with you; my peace I give you. I do not give to you as the world gives. Do not let your hearts be troubled and do not be afraid."

John 14:25-27

"Though I have been speaking figuratively, a time is coming when I will no longer use this kind of language but will tell you plainly about my Father. In that day you will ask in my name. I am not saying that I will ask the Father on your behalf. No, the Father himself loves you because you have loved me and have believed that I came from God. I came from the Father and entered the world; now I am leaving the world and going back to the Father." Then Jesus' disciples said, "Now you are speaking clearly and without figures of speech. Now we can see that you know all things and that you do not even need to have anyone ask you questions. This makes us believe that you came from God." "Do you now believe?" Jesus replied. "A time is coming and in fact has come when you will be scattered, each to your own home. You will leave me all alone. Yet I am not alone, for my Father is with me." I have told you these things, so that in me you may have peace. In this world you will have trouble. But take heart! I have overcome the world."

John 16:25-33

Romans:

Not only so, but we also glory in our sufferings, because we know that suffering produces perseverance; perseverance, character; and character, hope. And hope does not put us to shame, because God's love has been poured out into our hearts through the Holy Spirit, who has been given to us. You see, at just the right time, when we were still powerless, Christ died for the ungodly.

Romans 5:3-6

"For everything that was written in the past was written to teach us, so that through the endurance taught in the Scriptures and the encouragement they provide we might have hope."

Romans 15:4

May the God of hope fill you with all joy and peace as you trust in him, so that you may overflow with hope by the power of the Holy Spirit.

Romans 15:13

Therefore, there is now no condemnation for those who are in Christ Jesus, because through Christ Jesus the law of the Spirit who gives life has set you free from the law of sin and death. For what the law was powerless to do because it was weakened by the flesh, God did by sending his own Son in the likeness of sinful flesh to be a sin offering. And so, he condemned sin in the flesh, in order that the righteous requirement of the law might be fully met in us, who do not live according to the flesh but according to the Spirit.

Romans 8:1-4

I consider that our present sufferings are not worth comparing with the glory that will be revealed in us. For the creation waits in eager expectation for the children of God to be revealed. For the creation was subjected to frustration, not by its own choice, but by the will of the one who subjected it, in hope that the creation itself will be liberated from its bondage to decay and brought into the freedom and glory of the children of God.

Romans 8:18-21

We know that the whole creation has been groaning as in the pains of childbirth right up to the present time. Not only so, but we ourselves, who have the first fruits of the Spirit, groan inwardly as we wait eagerly for our adoption to sonship, the redemption of our bodies. For in this hope we were saved. But hope that is seen is no hope at all. Who hopes for what they already have? But if we hope for what we do not yet have, we wait for it patiently.

Romans 8:22-25

In the same way, the Spirit helps us in our weakness. We do not know what we ought to pray for, but the Spirit himself intercedes for us through wordless groans. And he who searches our hearts knows the mind of the Spirit because the Spirit intercedes for God's people in accordance with the will of God.

Romans 8:26-27

And we know that in all things God works for the good of those who love him, who have been called according to his purpose. For those God foreknew he also predestined to be conformed to the image of his Son, that he might be the firstborn among many brothers and sisters. And those he predestined, he also called; those he called, he also justified; those he justified, he also glorified.

Romans 8:28-30

What, then, shall we say in response to these things? If God is for us, who can be against us? He who did not spare his own Son, but gave him up for us all—how will he not also, along with him, graciously give us all things? Who will bring any charge against those whom God has chosen? It is God who justifies. Who then is the one who condemns? No one. Christ Jesus who died—more than that, who was raised to life—is at the right hand of God and is also interceding for us. Who shall separate us from the love of Christ? Shall trouble or hardship or persecution or famine or nakedness or danger or sword? As it is written, "For your sake we face death all day long; we are considered as sheep to be slaughtered."

Romans 8:31-36

No, in all these things we are more than conquerors through him who loved us. For I am convinced that neither death nor life, neither angels nor demons, neither the present nor the future, nor any powers, neither height nor depth, nor anything else in all creation, will be able to separate us from the love of God that is in Christ Jesus our Lord.

Romans 8:37-39

Be joyful in hope, patient in affliction, faithful in prayer.

Romans 12:12

May the God who gives endurance and encouragement give you the same attitude of mind toward each other that Christ Jesus had, so that with one mind and one voice you may glorify the God and Father of our Lord Jesus Christ.

Romans 15:5-6

1 Corinthians:

No temptation has overtaken you except what is common to mankind. And God is faithful; he will not let you be tempted beyond what you can bear. But when you are tempted, he will also provide a way out so that you can endure it.

1 Corinthians 10:13

2 Corinthians:

"But he said to me, "My grace is sufficient for you, for my power is made perfect in weakness." Therefore, I will boast all the more gladly about my weaknesses, so that Christ's power may rest on me. That is why, for Christ's sake, I delight in weaknesses, in insults, in hardships, in persecutions, in difficulties. For when I am weak, then I am strong."

2 Corinthians 12:9-10

Galatians:

"Let us not become weary in doing good, for at the proper time we will reap a harvest if we do not give up."

Galatians 6:9

Ephesians:

"For this reason, ever since I heard about your faith in the Lord Jesus and your love for all God's people, I have not stopped giving thanks for you, remembering you in my prayers. I keep asking that the God of our Lord Jesus Christ, the glorious Father, may give you the Spirit of wisdom and revelation, so that you may know him better. I pray that the eyes of your heart may be enlightened in order that you may know the hope to which he has called you, the riches of his glorious inheritance in his holy people, and his incomparably great power for us who believe. That power is the same as the mighty strength he exerted when he raised Christ from the dead and seated him at his right hand in the heavenly realms, far above all rule and authority, power and dominion, and every name that is invoked, not only in the present age but also in the one to come. And God placed all things under his feet and appointed him to be head over everything for the church, which is his body, the fullness of him who fills everything in every way."

Ephesians 1:15-23

"But because of his great love for us, God, who is rich in mercy, made us alive with Christ even when we were dead in transgressions—it is by grace you have been saved. And God raised us up with Christ and seated us with him in the heavenly realms in Christ Jesus, in order that in the coming ages he might show the incomparable riches of his grace, expressed in his kindness to us in Christ Jesus. For it is by grace you have been saved, through faith—and this is not from yourselves, it is the gift of God— not by works, so that no one can boast. For we are God's handiwork, created in Christ Jesus to do good works, which God prepared in advance for us to do."

Ephesians 2:4-10

"For this reason I kneel before the Father, from whom every family in heaven and on earth derives its name. I pray that out of his glorious riches he may strengthen you with power through his Spirit in your inner being, so that Christ may dwell in your hearts through faith. And I pray that you, being rooted and established in love, may have power, together with all the Lord's holy people, to grasp how wide and long and high and deep is the love of Christ, and to know this love that surpasses knowledge—that you may be filled to the measure of all the fullness of God."

Ephesians 3:14-19

"Now to him who is able to do immeasurably more than all we ask or imagine, according to his power that is at work within us, to him be glory in the church and in Christ Jesus throughout all generations, for ever and ever! Amen."

Ephesians 3:20-21

Finally, be strong in the Lord and in his mighty power.

Ephesians 6:10

Philippians:

"In all my prayers for all of you, I always pray with joy because of your partnership in the gospel from the first day until now, being confident of this, that he who began a good work in you will carry it on to completion until the day of Christ Jesus."

Philippians 1:4-6

Brothers and sisters, I do not consider myself yet to have taken hold of it. But one thing I do: Forgetting what is behind and straining toward what is ahead, I press on toward the goal to win the prize for which God has called me heavenward in Christ Jesus.

Philippians 3:13-14

I can do all things through Christ who strengthens me.

Philippians 4:13

Colossians:

Being strengthened with all power according to his glorious might so that you may have great endurance and patience, and giving joyful thanks to the Father, who has qualified you to share in the inheritance of his holy people in the kingdom of light.

Colossians 1:11-12

2 Thessalonians:

But the Lord is faithful, and he will strengthen you and protect you from the evil one. We have confidence in the Lord that you are doing and will continue to do the things we command. May the Lord direct your hearts into God's love and Christ's perseverance.

2 Thessalonians 3:3-5

And as for you, brothers and sisters, never tire of doing what is good.

2 Thessalonians 3:13

2 Timothy:

"For this reason I remind you to fan into flame the gift of God, which is in you through the laying on of my hands. For the Spirit God gave us does not make us timid, but gives us power, love and self-discipline."

2 Timothy 1:6-7

Hebrews:

We must pay more careful attention therefore, to what we have heard, so that we do not drift away.

Hebrews 2:1

Let us hold unswervingly to the hope we profess, for he who promised is faithful.

Hebrews 10:23

You need to persevere so that when you have done the will of God, you will receive what he has promised.

Hebrews 10:36

"Therefore, since we are surrounded by such a great cloud of witnesses, let us throw off everything that hinders and the sin that so easily entangles. And let us run with perseverance the race marked out for us, fixing our eyes on Jesus, the pioneer and perfecter of faith. For the joy set before him he endured the cross, scorning its shame, and sat down at the right hand of the throne of God. Consider him who endured such opposition from sinners, so that you will not grow weary and lose heart."

Hebrews 12:1-3

"Endure hardship as discipline; God is treating you as his children. For what children are not disciplined by their father? If you are not disciplined—and everyone undergoes discipline—then you are not legitimate, not true sons and daughters at all. No discipline seems pleasant at the time, but painful. Later on, however, it produces a harvest of righteousness and peace for those who have been trained by it."

Hebrews 12:7-8, 11

James:

"Consider it pure joy, my brothers and sisters, whenever you face trials of many kinds, because you know that the testing of your faith produces perseverance. Let perseverance finish its work so that you may be mature and complete, not lacking anything. If any of you lacks wisdom, you should ask God, who gives generously to all without finding fault, and it will be given to you."

James 1:2-5

Blessed is the one who perseveres under trial because, having stood the test, that person will receive the crown of life that the Lord has promised to those who love him.

James 1:12

1 Peter

"Praise be to the God and Father of our Lord Jesus Christ! In his great mercy he has given us new birth into a living hope through the resurrection of Jesus Christ from the dead."

1 Peter 1:3